So yo
WANT
to be a
DOCTOR?

CONTRIBUTORS

Medical Students
Glenda Ramirez

Residents
Anthony N. Harris, M.D., MBA
Dennis E. Bland, Esq., President
Center for Leadership Development, Indianapolis, IN
William Agbor-Baiyee, Ph.D., M.P.A., and Assistant Professor, IU
School of Medicine

Other Contributors
Sean Eugene Gardner, M.D., Anesthesiologist
Antoinette Austin-Glass, M.D., Anesthesiologist
Bettye-Jo Elvan Rawls Lloyd, M.D.
Lula P. Rawls

SO YOU WANT

WANT

to be a

DOCTOR?

A GUIDE FOR THE STUDENT FROM
HIGH SCHOOL THROUGH RETIREMENT

George H. Rawls, M.D.

Robert D. Patterson, M.D.

With a Foreword by Dr. Benjamin S. Carson, Sr.

HILTON PUBLISHING COMPANY
CHICAGO, ILLINOIS

© 2007 by George H. Rawls

Hilton Publishing Company
Chicago, IL

Direct all correspondence to:
Hilton Publishing Company
1630 45th Street, Suite 103
Munster, IN 46321
219-922-4868
www.hiltonpub.com

Library of Congress Cataloging-in-Publication Data

Rawls, George, 1929-
    So you want to be a doctor? : a guide for the minority student / George H. Rawls, Robert D. Patterson ; contributors, Anthony N. Harris . . . [et al.].
       p. ; cm.
    Includes bibliographical references.
    ISBN 0-9764443-3-X
       1. Medicine—Vocational guidance—United States. 2. Medical education—United States. 3. Minority students—Vocational guidance—United States. I. Patterson, Robert, M.D. II. Title.
       [DNLM: 1. Students, Medical—Personal Narratives. 2. African Continental Ancestry Group—Personal Narratives. 3. Education, Medical—Personal Narratives. 4. Education, Premedical—Personal Narratives. 5. Minority Groups—Personal Narratives. 6. Students, Premedical—Personal Narratives. W 18 R261s 2007]
    R690.R37 2007
    610.71'173—dc22   2006003450

Printed and bound in the United States of America

AUTHOR'S
ACKNOWLEDGMENTS

The authors would like to express their appreciation to the many people who have provided assistance in the publication of this book. First, to Ms. Furniss Holloway, for editing the manuscript, and to Bert Stern, Ph.D., Tom Woll of Hilton Publishing Company for their guidance during the publishing process. Thanks to Courtnye Rawls Lloyd and Jessica Williams for technical assistance, and Shangia Woods of the Indiana School of Medicine Foundation for assistance in typing and preparing the manuscript. Thanks to Dr. Jordan J. Cohen of the Association of American Medical Colleges for permission to use their rationale for supporting affirmative action and to use information pertaining to the MCAT. William Agbor Baiyee, Ph.D., contributed by describing the postgraduate Master of Science in Medical Science (MSMS) program at Indiana University School of Medicine (IUSM). Thanks to Antionette Austin-Glass, M.D., Bettye-Jo Rawls Lloyd, M.D., and Mrs. Lula P. Rawls, who served as contributing writers.

My gratitude goes also to Nancy Baxter of Guild Press Publishing of Indiana for permission to use information in *Papa, I Want to be a Surgeon*, to Deans Walter Daly, M.D., Robert Holden, M.D., and Craig Brater, M.D. Thanks also to Associate Deans James Carter, M.D., Herbert Cushing, M.D, and the administrators and faculty of IUSM for their help and for being the good colleagues they are.

Over the years, I have received helpful advice from Roland Smoot, M.D., of Johns Hopkins Medical School; Edward Helm, M.D., of Louisiana State University Health Science Center; and LaSalle D. Leffall, Jr., M.D., of Howard University.

Thanks to my many patients who taught me much about humanity, and to the physicians who referred them.

Finally, thanks to my parents and family, who inspired me and gave me support over the years. I dedicate this book to them.

CO-AUTHOR'S
ACKNOWLEDGMENTS

ROBERT D. PATTERSON

I would first like to thank my Lord and Savior, Jesus Christ, for the blessings and trials he has bestowed on me. I have been especially fortunate in my mentors and friends. To Dr. Rawls, I owe a lifetime of gratitude for his wise counsel and for inviting me to be the co-author of this book. Thanks to Dr. Benjamin Carson for his words of support and for writing the foreword for this book. Special thanks to Patricia Treadwell, M.D., Patricia Keener, M.D., Jerome Adams, M.D., Virginia Caine, M.D., Steve Bodgewic, PhD, Jose Espada, and Cynthia Holmes-Gardner. Thank you to Indiana University School of Medicine and all my professors for education received in and out of the classroom, and to Dr. Allan Tasman, Dr. Barbara Fitzgerald, Dr. Robert Frierson and the University of Louisville Psychiatry department for believing in me.

Thanks to my two closest friends Eric L. Mayberry and Cherrell Triplett, M.D., for their constant and loving support of me throughout my most difficult years. Special thanks also goes to Tracy Trass and family, Claude Taliaferro and family, the Chukwu family, Calvin Stroud, Sonya Hunt, my siblings, and my extended family in Gary, IN and Georgetown, KY who have provided support for me in the pursuit of my life's goals. Thank you to the Indiana University Student National Medical Association and the Indianapolis Aesculapian Society for providing me with opportunities to grow as an individual and as a leader.

To the angel of my life, Helen Valentine Chukwu, my pledge: You'll always be the center of my life.

Most of all I would like to thank my mother and father— Lorraine Wilson Patterson (deceased) and John Robert Patterson, who were the most dedicated and unselfish parents God has placed on this earth. Everything that is positive about my life has its roots in your soil, and every day I thank Him for being your son.

CONTENTS

Part III: Being a Doctor

Part IV: Social Issues and Solutions

FOREWORD

When I was in high school, and I would tell some of my classmates that I intended to become a physician, many of them would look at me with amazement and say "Don't you realize that you have to go to college for four years, and then to medical school for four years, and then do a year of internship and several years of residency? You will be an old man by the time you finish."

Interestingly enough, when I finished my residency, they were the same age as I. Therefore, time did not slow down for them simply because they chose to do something that required less time. You probably have youth on your side if you are reading this book, and you have some interest in pursuing a medical career. You should be aware that it is a long and grueling endeavor, and you have to learn an incredible amount of material. It has often been said that the first two years of medical school are similar to learning eight new foreign languages simultaneously in terms of the amount of material that must be mastered.

This does not even consider the fact that you first have to get into medical school which means having terrific grades in college which means not utilizing college as a social club, but rather as a ladder to climb to your goal.

Even though currently physicians must deal with long hours, stingy insurance companies, malpractice lawyers, and a host of regulatory agencies, they are still one of the few professions that can derive incredible satisfaction from what they do. People place in the hands of physicians their most valuable possession, namely, their lives, and we have the opportunity to extend those lives or improve the quality of those lives. It is a feeling that cannot be measured by money. However, one does need to recognize that if one is going to take on such enormous responsibility, one clearly has to be prepared. It is not a profession for those who like to shuck and jive and bluff their way through because the stakes are much too high.

This book really is a rather unique offering and shows a very young person the many steps and obstacles that they will face if they, in fact, want to pursue a career in medicine and uses personal stories in a very interesting way to bring home all the pertinent points that should be considered when considering a medical career. I want to add my thanks to the many others who appreciate the endeavors of the authors.

BENJAMIN S. CARSON, SR., M.D.
Director of Pediatric Neurosurgery
Professor of Neurological Surgery, Oncology, Plastic Surgery, and Pediatrics
Johns Hopkins Medicine

Part I

THE ROAD
TO THE M.D.

CHAPTER I

Should I Become a Doctor?

"Doc, you probably don't remember me, but you took my appendix out about twenty years ago." Now that I am retired, I often encounter former patients like this one when I go shopping or am playing golf. I seldom remember the person's name, but I do often remember the incident and circumstances. Encounters like these give me a sense of worth, achievement, and service to humanity. Whether I had gotten fully paid or whether I treated a patient out of a sense of service and received no pay did not matter. The essence of being a physician is in providing care, not in receiving payment.

For those who feel drawn to such service, years of tight discipline, lost sleep and an absent social life, even lost time with family, are all a part of the price. *So You Want to Be a Doctor?* sets out to look closely at why a person is drawn to such a path, and considers step-by-step how he or she pursues it. My subject obviously raises many questions: What is this path? How does one seek and find it? How does one remain on it? How does one balance his or her life to enjoy it? The passion to find answers to these questions must be the guiding passion of the would-be physician, just as it is the guiding passion of this book to provide the answers.

Coming to the Calling

When I was a boy of eight, after church, I would return home to become Reverend Rawls and preach to our chickens in the backyard. The next day, when the garbage man flexed his huge muscles and emptied our garbage can onto his truck, I wanted to become a garbage man. Another day, a fire truck went by, manned by uniformed, helmeted firemen in all their glory, or some neighborhood ruckus would bring forth a blue-clad policeman with his shiny badge, and again I would switch careers.

But by the time I was in my adolescence, pure fantasy ended and I began to look more seriously at the question of career. I decided that I needed help.

"Mom, what would you like for me to become?"

"George, become whatever you want to, but be a good one."

I harassed my mother with this problem for about a year. Finally, as if to silence me, she told me straight out, "I'd like to see you become a doctor."

A doctor, I thought. I had not considered that. *What do they do? How do you become a doctor? What would Papa say?* Papa was a chef and I always thought that he wanted me to become one, too. So I approached Papa a little hesitantly to see how he would accept my new goal. After all, he would have to pay the tuition bills.

I knew that paying for my education would not be easy. Although Father had always taken good care of us, he wasn't rich. Still, although he had only completed the sixth grade, he was a master at saving money and investing it wisely. He had bought land in Gainesville, Florida, and began building homes to rent. He learned rapidly and eventually directed the building of homes, though he continued to do much of the work. Papa built twelve homes over a few years and rented them. No, we were not rich but we lived comfortably. Papa had already decided that we all should go to college.

I approached him directly: "Papa, I want to be a doctor."

"A doctor? Why George, that's fine." Although I was only twelve, he immediately began to help me prepare to make my desire a reality. He sent away for catalogues to colleges and medical schools, and decided that I should attend Florida A&M for college and then go either to Meharry or Howard Medical School. At that time, Black colleges and medical schools were an almost inevitable choice for a young African American who aspired to be a doctor. So there it was: I was only twelve, but my father began then to save his money to pay for my education. I had found my course.

While I was in high school, my plans became even more real. One of my classmates, like me, wanted to be a doctor, and it turned out that his father was a doctor. My friend and I decided to get a job at Alauchia County Hospital to see what doctors do, so I quit my job delivering papers. At the hospital, my classmate washed pots and I washed dishes. I did not mind working in the kitchen. At least they fed me, even though the pay was lousy.

I gradually worked my way up to become a deliverer of patients' food trays. That is when I began to see sick patients. Some were in pain. Others slept. A few were frail. But their condition did not seem to bother me. Maybe that was because I was too young for that kind of sympathy. Or maybe it was then that I began to see sick people as people waiting to be healed.

I soon became a waiter in the doctors' dining room. The doctors were very kind and often asked me what I planned to do with my life. I would reply, "I am going to become a doctor." They became interested in me and would talk with me about what doctors do. That's when I knew I had found my way.

When I finished Lincoln High School, someone had put up a sign on a wall: "George is going away to become a doctor." Soon after I graduated, with a send-off gift of $200 in my pocket, I went off to college to pursue my dream.

That's the story of how I found my path, but there are a million others. For example, Janice Simpson, a medical school applicant worked as a research assistant at Pfizer Drug Company when she was a junior in high school. Her work was intriguing and challenging, and soon she set her goal to become a research medical scientist.

Randall Johnson received a degree in business and worked as a salesman at Eli Lilly & Company. His sales soared; and he was very successful. However, after a few years in sales Randall became eager to see how the drugs he sold helped patients get well. He began to take science courses and he enjoyed them. In his junior year, he did well on the medical school entrance exam, applied to medical school, and was accepted. Nontraditional medical students like Randall, because they are usually more mature and focused, tend to become excellent physicians.

Thomas Bowen's grandfather, father, and two uncles were physicians. What other career was Thomas to pursue but medicine? You'd think he was on the royal road, but it didn't turn out that way. He flunked out half way into his second year of medical school when he realized that he wasn't following his desire but his family's. Unfortunately, there are too many Thomas Bowens.

Of course, there are families like Thomas's in which a student receives positive influence from parents and/or relatives who are physicians. He is aware of the time commitment, the long hours of study, and the critical sacrifice of time spent with his family. He desires the genuine satisfaction of helping others, but he is realistic in his approach to medicine. He earnestly wants to become a doctor, but not because Dad or Mom is a doctor.

Yes, it is sad to see a student, often brilliant, who does not want to be a doctor but is "pushed" into it by parents because "it's in the family." There are also those sad cases in which Mom or Dad wants to be able to say, "My daughter (or son) is a doctor," and also may think, "She will make plenty of money and make us proud."

Woe befalls him or her who pursues medicine or any career primarily for monetary or other ulterior reasons. Often, the lack of a sincere desire to become a physician can be detected in the first interview at the medical school. The student subconsciously pleads with the interviewer to rescue him. Maybe he or she shows a lack of passion or answers a question with an "I guess so." Often such students feel relieved when they're turned down.

Sometimes the letters of recommendation themselves hint that a student might not be suited to medicine. The biology professor may hint at an alternate career for which the applicant is better suited. "Robert always wanted to be a marine biologist" is a pretty clear clue.

A student who gets through medical school despite having the wrong motivation can turn out to be a doctor who later gets into trouble either with the medical licensure board for not answering an emergency call, or, for repeatedly having a whiff of alcohol on his breath detected by the emergency room nurse. These kinds of misguided doctors may finally close the office and announce that they are going to do what they have always wanted to do—"become a musician." If you are in doubt about your own motives, your best bet is to take psychological tests to help determine whether you have the right motives and the necessary talents for becoming a physician.

Happily, most people who study medicine have a lot of good reasons. Perhaps a boy or girl was impressed by the care given to a sick family member. On the other hand, another may have been unimpressed by the care given and want to demonstrate that he or she can do it better. For others, a premed summer program ignites their interest and makes them think that they may have the right stuff to become physicians.

Yes, people come to medicine by a variety of paths, but what they have in common is that they feel called. Medicine isn't just a job—it is a calling.

CHAPTER 2

Preparing in High School and College

High school can be perilous to students' ambitions. Peer pressure can be a dominant influence, and it is often a distracting one. I recall Fred Motley, a neighbor's son. He had been a good student in elementary school, but in high school he sought popularity by snorting coke and drinking alcohol. His future was predictable unless there was a dramatic change. Sad to say, this change never occurred.

But for every such story there's a happier one. Alma Snorton, another high school student, studied, planned and prepared an excellent science project that won first place in the Science Fair. Then peer pressure went to work on her. Because she was now harassed and dubbed a "nerd" by her schoolmates, she no longer wanted to excel in her studies or pursue worthwhile projects for fear of being ostracized.

But Alma was luckier than Fred. Her parents worked diligently with her to overcome the stigma often imposed on good students. Alma herself began to think more seriously about her problem. It helped when her father told her: "Let me share my attitude: I like nerds. I admire nerds. And when it comes to choosing a doctor, I'd choose a nerd any day."

Once Alma no longer worried about ostracism, she found quite a few other "nerds" around her, and a more satisfying social life than before. She discovered also that, though motivated students are intensely focused on a goal or academic and career passions, they aren't one-dimensional. You, the motivated student who is reading this book, must keep in mind that, while becoming a doctor requires intense focus and dedication, you are a whole person. Being focused need not mean living in an academic prison. Instead, the curiosity and energy you take from your pursuit of a goal can help other aspects of your personality—relationship skills, affection for others, playfulness, self understanding, et cetera—to flourish.

High School

High school is where you should detect your strengths and weaknesses by asking yourself the following questions:

Do I analyze data well?

Do I retain and apply information?

Is my rote memory good?

Once you have come up with answers to these questions, you should try to accentuate positive attributes and work to strengthen them further. For the high school student who wishes to become a doctor, I recommend these practices:

- Enroll in as many science and math courses as possible.

- Learn not only the basic information but also the organizing and operating principles.

Back in high school, I had a friend, Earnest, who could memorize perfectly the laws of physics, but at first, did not know how to apply them. Then he discovered that although merely memorizing the laws might get him a good grade on one test, not understanding the principles would become apparent in the laboratory and hurt his overall performance.

A doctor is more than a medical computer. Yes, you need to feel comfortable with the sciences, but you also need to expand your diligence in studying to other courses, especially English, literature, speech and psychology. Courses like these give you different, less exclusively technical ways of understanding the world. They enhance your ability as a practicing doctor to understand others and yourself.

There are still other strengths that you will want to cultivate in high school:

- Learn to communicate well and to interpret the spoken and written word.

- Learn to write correctly and legibly.

- Try to become well rounded by participating in sports and other extracurricular activities. Remember that high school should be a memorable time in life, so enjoy it. Learning need not be a torture chamber.

- Participate in organizations and develop leadership attributes.

- Volunteer and give community service such as at hospitals and nursing homes.

- Review and study for the SAT and ACT tests. Take courses to prepare yourself for these tests if possible. Remember, you are competing against others who may be taking such courses.

Back in my day, when I asked teachers how I might prepare for such tests, they told me: "You *can't* prepare. Just get a good night's sleep." While getting a good night's sleep is a good idea, you *can* prepare by reviewing your high school studies, and preparatory courses help you to do that.

Naturally, not all your preparation will be academic. Ask your own doctor about her work, let her know of your interests, and ask if it might be possible for you to help her in the office to learn more about what a doctor does.

Start thinking about college. Visit and choose a college that has a strong science program—ideally, together with the English, literature, and psychology courses I mentioned above. You'll have a chance to talk to counselors about programs they offer for pre-med students who also want knowledge of the humanities and psychology. You'll also have a chance to meet students who are following the kind of program you wish to enter.

Don't be daunted by the fact that college costs a lot of money today; there are many scholarships available. Find out about them, and start filling out applications. With the help of your school counselor, or on your own, search out scholarships that may be available to you, and apply for them.

Once you begin taking these steps, you are on your way to college.

COLLEGE

Keeping in mind how especially demanding the requirements of medical school will be, develop good study habits while you are still in college. To be competitive for admission to medical school, you must have good study habits. In studying the sciences you will want not only to retain information, but also learn how to apply basic principles. While you will continue to take non-scientific courses, your focal point is to understand chemistry, biology, and physics, to retain information, and to learn how to apply basic principles. There are ways to help you learn:

- Attend all lectures.

- Take good notes.

- Listen well to those professors who, while lecturing, emphasize important points. (I have observed that this kind of professor gives almost 85 percent of his exam questions from his lectures. I realized back in medical school that I could almost write two-thirds of the professor's exam. He had prepared me that well.)

- Sit near the front of the class so you can hear the professor well.

- Visit the professor after class if you did not understand some of the lecture material. The professor will also get to know you.

- Make sure that the instructor knows who you are. Remember, you may need a recommendation from him or her.

- Scan notes and assignments frequently. Underline, read and then recite back important information to yourself.

- Join a small study group to go over study material and "bust each other out."
- Look over old exams, if available, and anticipate exam questions.
- Be curious and do research.
- Seek a quiet environment for study hours.

A college student, like a high school student, must develop leadership skills by participating in a few extracurricular activities. Admissions committees of medical schools look favorably upon leadership attributes. Nevertheless, unless you are exceptionally talented or brilliant, and perhaps even if you are, it's better not to overextend yourself in sports, choirs, bands, or Greek-letter organizations. It's always a question of finding the right balance.

Having said that, I'll remind you one more time—to get to medical school, you need to have a tight schedule of serious classes, and perform well in them. While the grade point average (GPA) isn't the only measure of a person's abilities, if you want to become a doctor you will need to maintain at least a 3.5 GPA especially in the sciences, and the GPA should be consistent from freshman to senior school years, and, ideally, steadily improve. The admissions committees like nothing better than to see a college applicant who had to struggle at first but overcame the obstacles.

While most professors want nothing more than to help you on your way, some may use harsh methods. At Florida A&M University, after I had been successful in two science courses taught by a professor I remember fondly, Dr. Anderson, and I had signed up to enroll in a third the following semester, he warned me, "You made As in each of my two courses, but if you enroll in physiology and do not do well, I will flunk you, so help me God." The lesson I learned from Dr. Anderson's warning was, "Don't let up. Don't think past successes guarantee future ones." Just like a football team, forget last week's victory; work to win the game you're now playing, course by course. Keep your eye on the ball.

THE MCAT

The Medical College Admission Test commonly referred to as the MCAT, may predict your ability to be successful in your first year in medical school. Most medical schools rely on it heavily in selecting students for their freshman class. While the MCAT changes over the years, its main emphasis is on the sciences: biology; inorganic and organic chemistry; and physics. There is also a section on verbal reasoning in which you are asked questions about a passage of writing. A score below eight on this section is suspect, and may suggest that the applicant may have a problem interpreting information. Each section is timed.

Just as I had been advised in high school that there was no way to prepare for the SATs, in college I was told the same thing about the MCAT. This is hogwash. You can, and should, prepare for it. Review all of your science courses. As in the case of the SATs, take a preparatory course if you can afford it. Many of your competitors will have taken one. If you are unable to take the course, there are preparatory books you can study. Just ask your librarian or local bookstore to help you find the right one for you.

Some students have the attitude, "I'll take it to see how it is." Unfortunately, that score may be the one used to evaluate you. Don't take that chance. Consider the first time the crucial one. You also need to determine the best time to take the test. A common mistake is to take the MCAT in April of one's junior year while taking physics and organic chemistry which are demanding courses. The result for the average student is predictable: His grades suffer and his MCAT score is below average.

I recommend that you first complete the junior year semester and do well in the science courses. At the end of your junior year, concentrate your studies on the MCAT that you will take in August. Some students take the MCAT in April, but they deprive themselves of the advantage of having a couple of months they can devote entirely to preparing for the MCAT. Don't consider the summer before your senior year as vacation time. Be ready, take the test, and *then* sleep "the sleep of the just."

Beginning in the year 2007, the MCAT will be administered solely by computer, which allows for more testing dates, a shorter overall test day, more controlled and standardized testing environments, quicker score reporting , and increased security.

For detailed information about the MCAT, see *www.aamc.org/ data/facts/start.htm*.

IN A NUTSHELL

- Qualifying for medical school begins in high school, if only because you know that, down the line, an admissions committee will be looking at your grades, along with the results of your MCAT.

- In high school, you'll want to start evaluating your powers of analysis, how well you retain and apply information, and discover the strength of your rote memory. Just by focusing on these qualities, you will have taken a step in the direction of improving them.

- In high school and college, take as many science courses as you can.

- Don't neglect courses like English composition and literature, speech and psychology. These courses, along with philosophy and history, help you better understand yourself and others.

- Review and study for the SAT and ACT tests, and take courses to prepare you for these tests if that is possible.

- While you are still in high school, think about which colleges can promise you a strong pre-medical education.

- Keep in mind that, while tuition is expensive, scholarships are available.

- In college, you will want to develop strong study habits.

- Maintain at least a 3.5 GPA, especially in the sciences.

- Diligently prepare for the MCAT.

CHAPTER 3

Applying to Medical School

Although some details may change from year to year, the basic rules are standard and simple. The student gets an application online from the AAMC (Association of American Medical Colleges), completes it, and returns it to the AAMC. The AAMC charges $150 for each application you submit. On average, students apply to seven to ten schools at a cost of $150 per school, which boils down to a total cost of anything from $1,050 to $1,500. (Yes, that's a chunk of money—a good reason why you should be saving your money in preparation for application time. Don't count on your parents to shoulder the whole load.)

Although you can apply as early as the spring of your junior year, the AAMC does not forward the application to the schools you've applied to until July. At that time each school further evaluates the application to see if the student is eligible according to its particular standards. Each school will probably require a supplementary application with an additional fee, the fee going this time to the school itself. While it is not necessary that you apply in your junior year, you should certainly apply by September of your senior year. The last day is December 15. However, many schools will have accepted many students into the freshman class by then.

The application process requires time. Not only must you fill out the application itself, but you must also obtain an official transcript from the college, along with the dean's letter indicating whether any legal action has been taken against you. Finally, you'll need several recommendations. By applying early, you have time to make sure that the dean and those who will recommend you have sent in their letters. Don't be shy about checking regularly to see whether the letters have gone out.

If there has been any legal or probationary action against you, admit and explain it. Otherwise the admissions committee of a medical school may question your integrity. No matter how impressive your GPA and MCAT may be, denial or evasion of your mistake will hurt you more than the mistake itself. I remember a student I'll call Josephine Munroe, who did not check the box that asked this question. In fact, when the dean reported her violation, she denied it. As a result, her admission to medical school was denied.

There is a good reason why admissions committees are concerned with your moral character. Medical licensure boards often find that doctors who have committed an offense that brings them under scrutiny turn out to have had problems in college, such as excessive drinking, but no one questioned them during the application process. By being open and frank about your offense, you show the members of the admissions committee that you, like many other human beings, have learned from your mistake. Of course, if there are repeated offenses or felonies in your past, you are likely to be rejected.

In a Nutshell

- Submit your application to AAMC in August before your senior year, thus leaving you with plenty of time to study.

- Be prepared to pay the expense of $150 per application.

- Respond to *all* the application questions. If there has been any legal or probationary action against you, admit and explain it. The committee will give you a chance to show that you've outgrown your mistake.

CHAPTER 4

The Interview

Having successfully completed the application process, you are now ready to convince an admissions committee that you should be one of the 16,000 applicants out of the total pool of about 40,000 or more who will be accepted into the 127 medical schools in this country. (Students with high GPAs and good recommendations can be interviewed first, and get a decision no later than October 1.)

How should you prepare yourself for the interview? Begin by researching the school, so that when you come to the interview, you bring with you a detailed understanding of the particular school itself. You might even do research on the work of one or two of the well-known scholars at the school you choose. This knowledge will also help you to ask specific and relevant questions.

For example, if you were applying to Indiana University School of Medicine, you would know that it is the second largest medical school in the country, that there are nine campuses to which the 280 students are assigned for the first two years, and that all of these students then do the final two years at the Indianapolis campus. You would also know that it is world renowned in its research and treatment of testicular cancer, hypertensive cardiovascular disease, and Alzheimer's disease. You would also know of its premier hospitals: Riley Hospital for Children, Wishard Hospital, Veterans

Administration Hospital, and Clarian Complex. Your knowing these facts shows committee members that you are willing to do your homework and that you have a genuine interest in the school.

Try to arrive on campus on the day before your interview, so you can get a good night's sleep. Appear for the interview well groomed and punctual. Once the discussion begins, it will help you to have a pleasant countenance and to look the person you are talking to in the eye.

You will be asked, and you will want to state clearly, why you want to become a physician. You obviously won't impress the committee if you answer, "Because doctors make plenty of money," or "I thought about being a lawyer, but I'm told that profession is over-crowded now," or "Both my parents and grandparents are physicians and I thought I should keep up the tradition." A genuine sense of calling is easily recognized.

The committee will also look for evidence that you have given real thought to your career choice, including thought about how to finance your education. It's a big plus for you if you have shadowed a physician to see what he or she does, or, through volunteer work at a hospital, if you have become familiar with the aroma of hospitals. You will also have a vision of what you want to be doing in ten or twelve years.

Of course, you will have questions for your interviewer also:

- Why did *you* become a physician?

- What is the failure rate of your students in classes and on the boards?

- What percentage of your students gets their first or second choice on the match for internship and residency?

Of paramount importance is the passion and candor that you demonstrate in your answers and your questions. If your grades dropped slightly and the committee asks you about that, have a sincere and honest answer. If your MCAT is below average, indicate that you plan to retake it—and mean it! Getting into medical school is a com-petitive endeavor. To the question: "*Suppose you do not get in, what will you do?*" you will have a well thought-out plan. You will not say: "I will go to dental school or veterinary school or physician's assistant school or nursing school." You will not say: "I plan to get a job in a hospital drawing blood or working as an orderly in surgery." At this stage, your answers should indicate your firm and informed determination to become a doctor. That determination includes finding ways past obstacles—even big ones, such as being rejected the first time you are interviewed for admission.

There are good answers to the question of what you will do if rejected. For example:

- I will have a counseling session with the chairman of admissions.

- I will enter a post-baccalaureate program or obtain a master's degree in one of the sciences and reapply next year.

Have a plan and be determined to become more competitive. That requires you to be steadfast and persistent. You don't have to be a genius to become a very good physician. You *do* need to work hard to become well-versed in the basic principles of medicine, and you cannot start that hard work too early.

A person who has been turned down by a medical school but is nonetheless determined to try again must be especially honest with himself. I will never forget Steve Mason. He worked hard in school; he studied, took notes, sought assistance, and kept his eye on his objective. While that focused work earned him fairly good grades in college, his score on the MCAT was a noncompetitive 16. Steve needed to get his MCAT score as far above 20 as he could to be competitive. Determined to know why hard work hadn't served him this time as it had in the past, he sought counsel and discovered that he had dyslexia. Did that deter him? Did he withdraw into a shell? No! Steve wanted more than anything to become a physician. He accepted the fact that he had a learning disability.

Steve Mason knew that it took him longer to do the reading than seemed necessary, and that had hurt his performance on the MCAT, since he didn't have time to complete the last section of the exam. He requested that he be allowed more time for his retake of the exam, and acted upon the recommendations of the psychologist who coached him. It took him two extra years of post-baccalaureate study, but he is now an anesthesiologist. And, he is a good one.

Steve kept his eye on the ball, and got through medical school to achieve his goal despite initial obstacles. If you follow the suggestions offered in this chapter, you too can win acceptance into medical school and be ready to "tackle the gator."

In a Nutshell

- Select four or five schools (keep in mind that state schools are usually less expensive.)

- Research each school and become familiar with the specialty for which it is most noted.

- Dress appropriately.

- Be on time.

- Be prepared to answer these questions:

    ~ Why do you want to become a doctor?

    ~ If you are not accepted, what are your plans?

    ~ Will you plan to retake the MCAT?

    ~ How will you finance going to medical school?

CHAPTER 5

Medical School

Medical school can be very stressful if you permit the experience to overwhelm you. But if you simply accept the fact that there is a tremendous amount of information to assimilate, and face it with confidence that what others have done you can do too, you will find it rewarding to discover just how much intellectual focus and capacity you really have.

While some of the subject matter will require that you understand the underlying principles and apply them, initially you'll need a great deal of pure rote memory. Sometimes, for all your willingness to work, the classes may feel crushing. Each subject is taught in detail and examinations are frequent. Furthermore, your classmates will be among the brightest students from the best colleges and universities in the world. No matter how good you are, there's almost always someone around who's a shade better. But do not despair. As I said, you don't have to be Einstein. Many students have done it and so can you. Do not become frustrated if you do not rank in the upper echelon of your class. Just always do your best.

Later, when you apply for a residency, your grades, class rank, and board scores will be considered in the selection process. That's why it's best to do as John Franklin did. He wanted to get off to a good start and not get behind from day one. He knew that if he were not ready for the challenge of professional school, he would be like the runner who was late breaking away from the blocks after hearing the starting gun.

John came a week early. He had been in contact with the financial officer since meeting him when he was interviewed. He had not gotten a scholarship though he applied to several sources. He considered enlisting in the armed forces, so that when he was discharged, his expenses and even a living allowance would be provided. But John feared the long delay that an enlistment would require. His dilemma was real. On the average, students owe $150,000 by the time they finish medical school. His parents would help but could not assume the complete burden. John decided on a loan.

By the time he began his first year of school, he'd done a lot of preparation. He'd planned a frugal budget that included making his own meals. He'd found a one-room apartment only 10 minutes from his classes. His dad had given him his three-year-old Chevrolet, so John had transportation. But he realized that he would not have time to get around much.

Before classes began, John had also visited the school to acquaint himself with the classrooms. He'd taken the medical school's pre-semester seminars on time management and on how to study. Finally, he had participated in the white-coat ceremony in which the dean or a representative puts a short white coat on the incoming student, and then exhorts students to study diligently, work hard, and become the best physicians they could be. When classes began, John felt ready to go.

I find that more recent students are less willing than John to live the spartan life their circumstances and phase of life dictates. I remember a recent student—call him Jamal—who came up to Indiana University School of Medicine for a summer seminar. Beforehand, he requested that we find living accommodations for him, and the administrator of housing was lucky to find an affordable, cozy, one-bedroom apartment on campus. After checking it out, Jamal remarked, "Unacceptable, totally unacceptable." Jamal wanted a two-bedroom apartment with dining room and living room, and found one in the city that met his requirements.

Many students today feel that they need a more-than-adequate apartment and an automobile. These extras obviously add greatly to the cost of education, but Generation X students will borrow the additional money to pay for them. From my own perspective, as an old codger who grew up during the Great Depression, such luxuries simply don't fit into the picture of being a medical student. But today they appear to be acceptable.

The First Year

The financial plan you made before entering medical school should have factored in that it's nearly impossible for you to work at an outside job while you are taking classes. You simply can't afford the time. I visited a first lecture in biochemistry a few years ago. At the end of the lecture, the professor distributed twenty pages of information. One student asked, "Is this all there is for the course?" "No," was the answer, "this is for today. Tomorrow there will be more." And tomorrow, and tomorrow.

Study material accumulates rapidly. The professor waits for no one. Courses during the first year usually include gross anatomy, biochemistry, molecular biology, histology, bacteriology, immunology, and physiology, or combinations of these with other basic sciences. The first series of exams may be given in two or three weeks. One or two may be given on the same day. And so it will go throughout. the year and the several years that follow.

Obviously, you need good notes. At some schools, a student is designated to tape and copy lectures and pass them out to classmates. If you miss a lecture—and that will be rare—taped notes are a great help. But I strongly recommend that you attend all lectures except when an illness or genuine emergency prevents you from doing so.

Some students take notes in class on 3 x 5 cards. This procedure requires a lot of time, and not many students are willing to use it, but those who do tend to do well in courses. There are also wrong ways to keep up with the rising river of new material to learn and to understand. Many students "ping pong"—that is, study only one course until exam time, then start studying for another course with the next scheduled exam for that course. But often two exams are scheduled for the same day.

I advised students to study each course daily, and then, for a few days in advance, to concentrate on the course or courses they will next be examined on. Even during that cram period you need to keep a grip on your other courses.

It can be a good thing for students to study together regularly by reviewing the subject matter and asking questions of each other. Naturally, this doesn't relieve you as an individual from the thorough understanding you'll need in order to be part of the discussion. In other words, such groups, besides sharpening your understanding of a subject, are strong motivators. If you are a student who came up through a bad school system, you may have to work twice as hard to catch up. You can do that extra work as long as you always keep in your mind's eye, your goal of becoming a doctor.

I suppose the best feature of studying with a group, besides the sense of community, is that you can correct your misunderstandings of the material. In a group study session I visited, a student gave a wrong answer to a question. A fellow student responded: "That's not the answer, Stupid. Can't you see what the answer is?" You may think that that this is a harsh way of correcting an error, but it can be the most effective one. It's not such a bad thing to be embarrassed about ignorance, as long as you immediately set about correcting it. A professor couldn't have used such a direct approach, but it worked well in this case. When the same question showed up later on an exam, the student knew the correct answer to the question.

Before an exam, review old ones. They will give you an idea of the potential parts of a question, and how it may be phrased. Further, knowing the answers to questions on old exams will also help you answer questions on the new one.

If there's something you don't understand before an exam, see the professor. In any case, it's a good idea to make certain that the professor knows you. Yes, professors can be intimidating, but they're human. Rightly or wrongly, they may sometimes even give special consideration in grading to a student who had come by several times and shown real interest in his studies.

THE SOPHOMORE YEAR

The most dramatic change in the second year curriculum is the introduction of a course in pathology. In that course you will learn in detail the special qualities of every disease. This is obviously a tall order. To make matters still more interesting, the early writers of medical information, some of whom you need to depend on, may not have used a common system of naming tissues or diseases. For example, I remember being asked the name of the cancer which originates from the lining of the stomach. What else could it be except "columnar cell carcinoma?" After all, the cancer originating from the skin was "squamous cell carcinoma." These were the common cells of origin. But the early icons preferred to name the cancer of the stomach according to the glands that the cells formed, hence, *adenocarcinoma*. As you can see, answering the question isn't as easy as it looks, because there is no uniformity naming the particular cancer at the heart of the disease.

To make matters still more complicated, diseases were often named after physicians who discovered them or made significant contributions to our understanding of them. If there were several contributors, each may have his name attached to the disease. For example, over-activity of the thyroid may be called "Graves disease," "Basedow's disease" or "Parry's disease." The term *thyrotoxicosis* may also be used. Although, eventually, the student will get to know each of these eponyms, he or she may be confused when first asked to identify Parry's disease.

The complexities of medical knowledge certainly are daunting. Take comfort in the fact that the playing field is level. Everyone faces all the same puzzles.

By the sophomore year, you should have developed good study habits and learned to manage time well. However, some students still need to learn. Dallas graduated from Indiana University with a GPA of 3.5, and he had done well on the MCAT. He came in to see me when I was assistant dean at Indiana University School of Medicine (IUSM). He had failed the first pathology quiz. I reviewed his study habits and discussed with him his management of time. Dallas's account of his study time seemed perfectly correct until we came to

Tuesday. I asked what he studied first on Tuesday evenings. "Nope, I don't study on Tuesday; that's our night out," he answered. I asked him to explain and he went on: "My significant other and I always take Tuesday and Saturday nights," he explained.

"You cannot do that in professional school," I suggested. "You must study on Tuesday night just like on every other night."

"She'll get mad and leave."

"Please take my advice this one time and let's see how you do on the next path quiz."

He returned in two weeks with a broad smile on his face. "You know, you were right," he said. "I made 97 on that exam. I am going to start studying on Tuesday nights. She *did* get mad, but when I explained why this was so important she understood." You also will need your Tuesday nights, and maybe Saturday nights as well.

Dallas has now completed his residency in internal medicine, has a master's degree in public health, and is practicing internal medicine. I don't know, but I hope he is going with the same girlfriend. She showed her love by allowing him the time he needed for his studies.

THE JUNIOR YEAR

The time finally arrives when you begin to feel like a doctor. In your freshman and sophomore years you will have seen a few patients from time to time and will have discussed their illnesses. Now you will see them daily. Patients become teachers as the student learns how to care for the sick. You become part of the team although you're at the bottom of the totem pole. You know that one day you will trade in your short coat for a long one and become an intern, then a resident, chief resident, and finally the attending physician who commands the post and approves all major decisions regarding the care of the patient. Until then, you will often have to do the "grunt work," such as taking a patient's history and physical, drawing blood, or holding the retractors in surgery for many hours. A junior student who was part of my surgery team, after four hours of pulling on a retractor, lost his attention and scratched his nose. Much to the joy of the student, I merely chased him out of the operating room.

In the junior year, you will have to make several important decisions. When I was in medical school many years ago, students didn't have to decide on a specialty until they were well into their internships. Now, the decision must be made in March of the junior year, and it will determine in which residency program and hospital you work. There is some leeway: You can apply for, and be matched with, a "provisional internship." In that way, you can delay your final decision regarding specialty training until you have a good taste of the kind of specialty in which you may settle. The disadvantage of a provisional internship is that you may later be competing with students who made their decision at the outset. It may be more difficult for you to enter the specialty, or to be assigned to the hospital of your choice. It's not an easy decision, but you will have to make it.

Naturally, not all junior-year students are sure which specialty—family practice, psychiatry, or one of the many other specialties—they want to pursue. I remember a student who was certain that neurosurgery was his calling. But by the time he had completed a five-year neurosurgical residency, he began to realize that strokes, with their frequent aftermaths of non-responsive patients, can be depressing to caregivers. Working with stroke patients certainly depressed him.

He then took a residency in general surgery and did very well, but he was still uncertain what kind of surgeon he wished to be. A resident in general surgery gets a taste of the wide selection of fields within the discipline of surgery itself. For this student, the field in which he found his niche was cardiac surgery. After the four-year general surgery residency, he completed a fellowship in cardiac surgery and became an outstanding heart-transplant surgeon.

I don't have to go far afield for examples of medical students who *did* change their minds. My daughter, Bettye-Jo, planned to be a pediatrician—until she discovered that she was not comfortable working with non-communicative patients. She was bothered by the fragility and smallness of babies, especially premature ones: "The babies are so tiny," she exclaimed. "You can hold them in one hand." It was not until she rotated on ophthalmology that she discovered her true specialty. She was fascinated with the diseases and disorders of the eye and with their treatment. Besides, she said, "The patients can talk to you. They are usually not really sick, and you need to care for the eye only and not the whole body."

There's another important decision to be made in the junior year: "Do I want to do academic medicine or community medicine?" In the first case you're most interested in teaching medicine, in the second, in practicing it. Training programs may be geared toward one or the other. If in doubt, you should assume that you may do academic medicine and apply to hospitals with strong academic programs. But of course, many hospitals prepare the community physician with excellent training, and you may prefer to apply to one of them. Choices! Choices! Choices! Decisions! Decisions! Decisions! But that's how life is.

In your junior year, you will start rotation, which means that you will get some hands-on experience in subjects ranging from pediatrics and obstetrics/gynecology to surgery. You will receive grades for each rotation, and some students who were only average in class work earn honors as they begin to work with patients. Here's how *you* can do that. First, work up each patient completely. Mine is an extreme case, but my first history and physical write-up, commonly referred to as the H&P, was thirty-five hand-written pages. On the physical exam, I covered every conceivable symptom in detail as well as every organ system. During the thirty-four years that I was in practice, it might appear that I reduced my H&Ps one page per year, because in my thirty-fourth year, my H&Ps were one page in length. But, in fact, I began to decrease the pages early in my practice.

A second way to earn honors while you're doing rotations is to dictate the H&P promptly and then write a brief note covering the most important features on the H&P. A third is to be prompt for ward rounds and surgery. Fourth, read the textbook about the diseases assigned to you. Fifth, take notes on ward rounds as well as grand rounds. Ward rounds are visits to patients on the ward confined to bed. Grand rounds means a conference of students and doctors to discuss a specific case.

Review your notes periodically throughout the semester, and again before the written exam that most attending physicians or residents give. If you are on pediatrics rounds, be sure to read and learn about growth and development. Pediatric professors are sure to examine your knowledge of this subject.

DEATH AND DYING

While a doctor's aim is to save lives, some patients die, and it is in your junior year that you come face to face with this hard fact. I remember once repairing an inguinal hernia on an elderly gentleman, during the days when hernia patients remained in the hospital for seven days until their stitches had been removed. He did fine until the day of his discharge, when he got up to go to the bathroom and fell to the floor dead. The cause of his death turned out to be a blood clot in the leg that broke loose and traveled to the lungs (pulmonary embolus), causing immediate death. I had indicated to the family beforehand that this complication could occur, but of course they were devastated when it happened.

Blood clots in the legs are one of the most dreaded complications of surgery, occurring usually on the fifth to seventh day after the operation. The patient is doing well, is ambulatory, and then succumbs while walking. Even though today we get patients to walk early, and provide stockings for compression where necessary, some patients succumb. As a doctor, you have to learn to live with this fact.

Death, especially sudden death, has always been a mystery to me. But death is also a fact: We must all die, whether of a lingering illness or suddenly. When doctors are performing procedures that carry risk, they need to explain this to both the patient and the family. Otherwise, the doctor may be liable. But it is, above all, a moral duty.

While sudden death can be hard for doctors to explain and for families to accept, counseling the patient and family in cases of slow death from a lingering disease or condition can be still harder. Slow death occurs especially in patients with cancer. While it is easy to "know" that we all must die, most of us don't think about death. We live as though we were immortal and we avoid the thought that we will cease to be.

Of course, many schools of thought assure us that even death is not absolute. Some scientists say that we vanish or decompose as persons but our molecular particles live forever. Christians believe that the soul lives on in an afterworld of paradise for the good and hell for the bad. Buddhists propose that we are subject to incarnation, either upward or downward in consciousness, and are thus immortal.

But for all those possible comforts, when the time comes, most of us still seem to believe that, while others may die, our own death sentence is abrupt and unfair. Yes, death is unfair, but it is universally unfair. None of us is an exception. We are all equal in death. There is no right time. We are not too busy, or too young. Death may come at any time.

A special problem we doctors face with death is that we may think of it as our failure. We work to keep people alive as long as we can. We even insert feeding tubes to keep vegetative or essentially dead people alive. If a patient dies, we often review his or her case to see if we did something wrong. While reviewing cases is a good way to learn from mistakes, if they happen, and experiences, we must accept that sometimes people just die.

Strictly from the physician's point of view, death is a medical process. Breathing ceases. The heart stops pumping blood. The brain refuses to react to stimuli. But death is also a divine secret, and I pray that it will remain so. Of course, as we learn more and more about the human body, some scientists believe that we may someday solve the mystery of death, and even eliminate it. Heaven forbid! Our species isn't ready to "manage" death. Human beings aren't meant to wield the power of gods. That is why I rejoice that death remains a divine mystery. It is my own hope that it is intertwined with eternal life.

In your junior year you must begin to work these problems out. Above all, you must learn to relieve pain and suffering, even where a cure is impossible. You need to be capable of compassion and willing to allow the time necessary to discuss with patients and families the great emotional wound brought on by the death of a loved one.

WORKING WITH OTHERS

The junior year student must learn to work with, and respect nurses, aides, therapists, orderlies, and technicians, for they too are important members of the health team. More than once I've learned important lessons from members of my team. For example, a woman came in complaining of lower abdominal pain, and my first thought was appendicitis. But a nurse who noticed how unusually pale the patient was suggested the possibility of an ectopic pregnancy—that is, a pregnancy outside the cavity of the uterus. After we examined the patient more closely, the nurse was proved right, and the next day we rushed the patient to surgery for an ectopic pregnancy.

Legal Documents

You must also become acquainted with two legal documents that all patients should complete and sign. The first is the living will declaration, also known as the physician's directive. Such a directive indicates what kind of care a patient wants when he or she is no longer able to make medical decisions—for example, if the patient has an illness from which he or she is not likely to recover, or becomes permanently unconscious. The signed directive prevents terrible legal struggles between family members over whether or not the doctor should keep an unconscious patient alive through the use of extreme measures. For example, a living will would have prevented the case in Florida in which a woman's parents were locked in a long legal struggle with her husband about whether to keep the unconscious woman alive through the use of IVs and oxygen. Had she signed this form, the bitter battle might never have started.

Another important document is the health care representative form. This form allows the representative to make medical decisions the patient is no longer able to make, and provides a clear description of the authority the patient is willing to give to the representative.

Communicating with Patients

In the junior year, you will learn to give specific, clear instructions to patients. Keep in mind that any lapse on your part can cause harm to the patient. I recall vividly a patient who returned to the hospital a day after being discharged. I had done a circumcision on him. When he came in, his penis looked as if it had been put through a meat grinder. It turned out that I had not explicitly told him not to have sex and he went ahead and did.

After that episode, I gave complete instructions, most of them written, to all my patients. Some doctors think that it makes no sense giving instructions because the patient may not be smart enough to follow them. I think that's a serious mistake. If you've tried to keep the instructions as simple and clear as you can and still failed to get them across, give written instructions so that a family member or a friend of the patient will be able to explain them.

THE SENIOR YEAR

You are now rapidly becoming a physician and taking on more responsibility. You will also have more choices. You will want to obtain a rotation in a hospital and in the specialty that is your first choice. You can achieve this by:

- Doing your work well

- Making sure the chief of the service and chief resident know who you are

- Displaying enthusiasm and participating in discussions about patients

- Reading intensively about the specialty of your choice

- Asking to be called for emergencies or interesting cases— even if it is your night off

- Being present for procedures like insertion of catheters (intravenous and bladder), nasogastric, and gastric tubes

- Learning basic surgical techniques like suturing and tying of square knots.

Remember that you will be given an exam on each rotation, so prepare as you did in your junior year. In addition, you must take and pass Part 2 of the USMLE at most institutions. The USMLE is the United States Medical Licensing Exam, and you need to study for it early. Without passing the exam, no matter how well you did in other aspects, you cannot graduate from most medical schools. You can find sample questions at *www.medstudents.com.br/exam/exam2/frame2.htm*.

Some schools require special competencies of students—for example, communication skills and legible handwriting. I remember a senior student who had passed all his courses but didn't know how to communicate with patients or the attending staff. In addition, his notes on charts were illegible and disorganized. His final grades and graduation were delayed until he learned to correct these deficiencies.

Oral and written communication skills are part of a doctor's humanity. Dr. Stephen Leapman, Professor of Surgery and Executive Associate Dean for Educational Affairs at Indiana University School of Medicine, remarked in an article in the *Indianapolis Star* (November 6, 2002) that "humanism must be the integral underpinning of education; nowhere is that more apparent than in medicine."

Dr. Leapman concluded that "a competent member of society is . . . one with character, morals, and high ethos. Recognizing that these traits are not innate but can be taught, assessed, and then practiced is the first step in formulating appropriate higher educational curricula." The first students to graduate under this modified curriculum distinguished themselves not only by bringing information about cleanliness and prevention to the community; they went *into* the community and helped clean yards. We are optimistic that physicians of the future will be more compassionate and more willing to tackle the basic environmental conditions that make for sickness or health.

In a Nutshell

- Attend a pre-matriculation program if one is offered.

- Develop good time management skills.

- Develop good study habits.

- Participate in small study groups.

- Attend classes, take good notes, and study your notes.

- Prepare adequately for exams.

- Do not ping-pong (study only one subject as you prepare for exams).

- If you don't understand a concept or procedure, seek help early from the professor.

- If you are called before the promotion committee, study the plan outlined by Robert Patterson in the next chapter.

Graduation

The day for which you've sweated and sacrificed has finally arrived. Graduations, like births and weddings, are rites of passage—exciting because they mark the beginning of a new life. Graduation day is a day for exuberance, laughter, embraces, kisses, and tears of joy.

If you have successfully followed the path this book maps out for you, you will have graduated with honors and will be looking forward to a premier residency. If you've managed to graduate, but without honors, well, you've graduated. It's no time now to say, "I could have done that. I should have done that."

If you've succeeded at doing your best, you'll come to graduation day with high hopes and no regrets. With your passion to serve and fire in the belly to learn, you are now ready to give compassionate and expert service to mankind. It may be in delivering your first baby unassisted, and hearing the mother's cry of pain with each contraction transformed to cries of joy.

So many visions rise up from a graduating class of new doctors. One person may now dream realistically of extending lives by transplanting a kidney or lung or heart or liver. Another anticipates feeling the warm return of a child's smile after properly diagnosing and treating her infected tonsils. Satisfactions to come could be relieving the pain of a patient with a broken leg by splinting it, or helping a psychotic patient return to reality through the use of the right medications. The ways a doctor may be of use are virtually endless.

At graduation, there is always a speaker who will challenge you to go forth into the world to give such service. At my own graduation from Howard University School of Medicine in 1952, the speaker was President Harry Truman, and I'll never forget the event. A tall, tanned man was blocking my view of the President, and when I requested that he move, he only smiled. I learned later that he was a Secret Service agent there to protect the President.

The ceremony over, you can look forward to the future with happy anticipation. You are about to embark on a journey of service, love, and satisfaction. You can also look forward to taking a few weeks off before beginning your internship. You've earned them. You may even find that this is a moment when you can look backward at your years in medical school with a calm satisfaction.

Part II

Reflections of Students, Residents, and Other Physicians

CHAPTER 6

Overcoming Obstacles

Robert D. Patterson, M.D.

The road to and through medical school generates thousands of stories each with its own account of obstacles met and overcome, of anxiety and triumph. Here is one such story by Robert D. Patterson, M.D., who, at the time of this writing, was a fourth-year medical student and President of the Student National Medical Association (SNMA), Indianapolis Chapter. His story will give you a unique perspective on the process of becoming a doctor.

I am not your typical medical student, if any such exists. Not only am I older than most, but I already had had one career before I entered medical school.

I was brought up to think of success as reaching "my level." It wasn't about achievement for achievement's sake; it was about effort and desire. I also learned to believe that if you truly and steadily try your hardest, you will succeed at whatever you go after. I never read or heard anything that spelled out this philosophy until, the Reverend Jesse Jackson gave his address before the Democratic National Convention, while I was still in college. As he talked of his plans for proceeding into the future, he recited a poem by an unknown author:

I'm tired of sailing my little boat far inside the harbor bar.
I want to go out where the big ships float,
out on the deep where the great ones are.

And should my frail craft prove too slight
for the waves that sweep those billows o'er,
I'd rather go down in a stirring fight
than drown to death on the sheltered shore.

Those words have been my beacon ever since.

When I heard from my football coach that I'd won a scholarship to college, my parents were as excited as I, but they encouraged me to pray about my decision, keeping my goals in mind. During that period of prayer, my thoughts ran like this: DePauw University, to which I'd won the scholarship, had a strong academic reputation, along with classes small enough so that students could get individual attention. Second, I am Black and, to this point, had mostly lived within a Black community. DePauw had only a small minority population, and I knew that it would help me to improve my skills at communicating with the larger community. Third, to attend college, I needed a full scholarship, and that is what the DePauw coach offered me. My last consideration was that I had a very strong relationship with all of my family, particularly with my mother and father, and I didn't want that to change. Happily, DePauw was only a two-and-a-half hour bus ride from my home in Gary, Indiana. After a night of prayer, the decision had been made for me—I would attend DePauw University in the fall.

When I got to the campus for freshman indoctrination, I was excited, but I was also apprehensive. There were only five African Americans in my class that year and only twelve in the entire university. The high school I'd gone to had been largely Black, but the bottom line was the same: Whatever the racial mix, I could compete. I was used to hard work.

Early in my first season, I decided that playing football was no longer important to me. College football is much more like a job than high school football, and I missed the camaraderie I'd shared with my high school buddies. On the Saturday morning when I met with Coach to inform him of my decision to leave the football team,

I was afraid that he would be upset—especially since he'd made sure that all my tuition expenses had been paid for as he had promised. I was also worried that my decision to leave the team violated my own unwritten rule about not quitting something once I'd begun. But Coach was very understanding, and promised me that as long as I performed at an acceptable level academically, DePauw would continue to provide the financial support I needed.

I was in a different phase of my life now, one strictly dedicated to my academic pursuits, and I was excited about my possibility for success. As I prepared my schedule for my first semester, I tried to imagine how each course would help bring me closer to the job opportunities I desired in the future. The only problem was that I had no idea what I wanted to do with my life.

So I sorted out the possibilities. I had always found the law interesting, and I also toyed briefly with the idea of being a sports agent. But in the end, I decided on a career in business and designed my schedule around the pursuit of that goal. DePauw University, as a liberal arts school, offered no business major. The closest one could come to it was a major in economics, so I took as many courses in that field as I could. I also took a lot of political science, literature, and philosophy classes, and actually finished with a minor in the latter.

There certainly wasn't much in my class schedule that pointed toward a career in medicine, but I hadn't given any serious thought to becoming a doctor. I had found science and math subjects interesting in high school, but not interesting enough for me to pursue at the college level. The only science course I took during my four years at DePauw was a class in geology—and I took it only because a science course was a requirement for graduation.

In May of 1988, after four very challenging years, I received my bachelor's degree from DePauw University with a major in economics. My plan to dedicate myself strictly to my academic success went well, and I graduated from college in the traditional four years with a GPA of 3.23. In fact, I had done so well that I was offered, and accepted, an opportunity to study off-campus during the first semester of my senior year in Philadelphia, an experience that would become significant in my future career plans.

Graduation was a very special day for my family because I was the first member on either my maternal or paternal side to graduate from college. It was also great for me because, unlike many graduates, I was certain about my next step. While I was in Philadelphia, I attended a conference of the Black Master's of Business Administration Association (BMBA). At the time, the MBA was receiving a lot of press as being a "hot" degree. Graduates from top ten MBA programs were almost always guaranteed very lucrative compensation packages from future employers and would generally be slated for the "fast-track" career path within the company that hired them.

In 1989, I was selected as one of only fifty awardees of the Consortium Scholarship in the United States. I was accepted for admission to several top business schools out of state, but I chose once again to stay close to home, so I accepted admission to Indiana University's Graduate School of Business (IUGSOB) in Bloomington, ranked as one of the top programs in the country.

I was active in student life while I pursued my MBA and, as a resident assistant (RA) for one of the undergraduate dormitories, I enjoyed the responsibility and social interactions with the undergraduates in my charge. I also enjoyed the opportunities to mentor them.

SUICIDE

Then, in my second year as an RA, one of the students who lived on my floor committed suicide by hanging himself. While the event in itself was devastating enough, it was made worse by the fact that I was also the one who discovered the body. The horrible visual memory of that has not left me to this day. I had steered a steady course toward my goals until then, but I felt somehow responsible, and the weight of my guilt drained me emotionally.

Despite this, I kept studying for finals, against the wishes of my family and friends, who worried about my emotional state. I thought that if I focused on my studies I could keep the images of that day from the forefront of my memory. My strategy didn't work very well, and a few nights before the beginning of my finals, I placed an emotional telephone call to the office of the Dean of Students. The Dean was very accommodating, allowing me to take my finals two weeks later. Sadly, the delay didn't help much. I didn't perform well, but given the circumstances, passing all my courses and graduating was a successful outcome.

So there I was, MBA in hand, and, as luck would have it, I got a job as a salesman for Eli Lilly & Company, whose headquarters are in Indianapolis. Looking back, I see that this was my first step toward a career in medicine. At the time, it was simply a choice job with one of the largest and most successful pharmaceutical companies in the world. My sales territory was one of the most economically depressed parts of the country—Paterson and Passaic, New Jersey. Each morning, I'd leave my comfortable suburban apartment to spend my day in an area that God seemed to have forsaken. I felt great satisfaction to be bringing, by way of my samples of new drugs, some comfort into these communities, but each evening, as I returned home, I felt guilty. I could be doing more, something inside kept telling me.

I felt a close identification with this area in New Jersey because it reminded me of Gary, Indiana, where I had grown up, and where, as here, access to medical treatment was poor. In both parts of the country there were good, caring doctors, but there weren't enough of them. In waiting rooms there were always more patients than seats, with sick people spilling out into the halls. Yet, no patient dared leave, because it could be many weeks before they could get another appointment and they were sick now. I remembered these scenes from my childhood, and I was reliving them now.

What I enjoyed best about the job was working with physicians. The majority of them were true humanitarians, emotionally invested and determined to provide a better quality of life to their patients.

Yet, for all my satisfaction and interest in the job, and despite the fact that I was good at it and was paid well, in the end the job did not satisfy my thirst for a still deeper spiritual purpose.

SEVEN HABITS

That's when my best friend, Eric Mayberry, suggested that I read a book by Stephen R. Covey entitled, *The 7 Habits of Highly Effective*

People, a spiritually-based book that gave me my mission statement: "Continual evolution toward the purest level of my spirit according to the will of God." (*The 7 Habits of Highly Effective People*, published by The Free Press, A Division of Simon & Schuster, 1989). In the following weeks, through continual prayer, I came to realize that to become a medical doctor was the best possible way for me to act out my goal; I would become a doctor and grow spiritually through my practice. From that point, I needed only to set out on my journey.

———————————————

One of the first things I learned, or had reinforced, was that my journey would carry me into obstacles and through them. Faced with the medical school's requirement that to be admitted, a student needed to pass two semesters each in inorganic chemistry, organic chemistry, biology, and physics, I entered the premedical program at Northwestern University. The program gave me the scientific knowledge and understanding I needed for admission.

One of the things that helped me fight my way through medical school was my desire for a practice in which I knew each patient personally, so that I could help them emotionally, spiritually, and physically. Part of this dream was that I would also be able to teach my patients the art of prevention, so that they would live longer and healthier lives.

In part because of pressure from insurance companies and in part because of doctors' large practices, healthcare has become an increasingly depersonalized trend. I wanted, in my small way, to help change that. The focus has moved from one-on-one physician/patient relationships to a system in which a patient can visit the same medical practice on different occasions and never see the same doctor twice.

The truth is this sense of my medical mission started much earlier. I knew a wonderful lady whose mother, and then an older sister, died of cancer at an early age. The lady herself was haunted by the thought of dying of the disease. She was not sophisticated to the level of using the Internet and medical journals to understand the diagnostic tests that she ought to have been given to check for early signs of cancer. Those tests might have meant early and successful treatment that could have alleviated her fears. Instead, she did what a lot of us do—she put her faith in her doctors.

From the age of forty-five on, she visited a doctor every six weeks—eight to nine times a year—and because of her type of health insurance, she saw many different doctors during her frequent visits. Seven years after she began these visits, she was diagnosed with metastatic colon cancer. Inoperable, it had spread throughout her body—to her liver, lymph nodes, everywhere.

She Died

She died on October 17th, of the same year, two-and-a-half months after the diagnosis, and she was laid to rest on October 21, 1997.

That wonderful lady was my mother.

A simple fecal occult test, which should be given annually to all men and women over the age of 50, could have detected the cancer in time to remove it before it had begun to spread. My point here is not to criticize the physicians who handled my mother's care. Physicians are human, and mistakes are a part of human nature. But truly adequate healthcare requires a consistent and trusting interpersonal relationship between physician and patient. Such care is best provided by the community-based, family practice physician. Had my mother been provided with that kind of watchful, personal care, she needn't have died.

My mother's death confirmed my conviction that along with scholarship, discipline, perseverance, and industriousness, physicians need a sense of duty and a compassionate heart for their patients. I knew that I had these qualities, and I encourage you, the reader, to take a continual inventory of your life and your expectations for the future as you pursue this noble profession.

During my first year at Indiana University School of Medicine (IUSM) I encountered serious academic difficulties: I failed both gross anatomy and histology. Subsequently, as is the procedure at all medical schools, my academic performance was reviewed by a board of professors and physicians charged with overseeing students' academic progress. They scheduled a time for me to meet with them to discuss my academic failures.

To say that I was nervous would be an understatement. I was determined that my journey not end here, after I had made many personal and professional sacrifices to gain acceptance at the age of 33. I was eager to express to them my renewed commitment to being a successful student, but I had little guidance on how to approach the situation. I walked into the meeting with no plan, written or unwritten, for how I could approach this meeting in such a way as to earn a second chance.

As I entered the room, I saw what I perceived to be concern on the faces of the professors and physicians in the room. The chair of the Promotions Committee introduced me to the board and outlined the academic failings that had led to their review. They then gave me as much time as I needed to explain the reasons behind my sub-par performance, but I used only a few minutes to declare, "I can do better." Then the members took turns asking me very specific questions about "how" I would do so.

I wasn't able to answer these questions to the Committee's satisfaction, because I'd failed to think in detail about how to correct my problem. As a result, I received the most shocking email of my life: "We regret to inform you that the Committee has voted to dismiss you from the school of medicine effective immediately."

I called the assistant dean responsible for students who had appeared before the Committee. She had previously explained to me that students who failed two courses were generally given an opportunity to repeat the first year of classes. What had happened in my situation? While she had no concrete answer to that, she did offer me three alternatives: 1) Forget about medical school and pursue a career that better fit my skills, 2) Contact the few U.S. and foreign medical institutions that will consider students who have been dismissed from other medical institutions, or 3) Make an appeal to the Promotions Committee for reinstatement. I knew at once that for me, the appeal was my only real option.

Immediately I resolved not to make the same mistake I had made in my first appearance before the Committee. I would swallow my pride and contact as many students as I could for advice about preparing for my next meeting. I also sought the help of my mentor, Dr. George Rawls, and of several other professors and physicians.

Some of those I contacted were familiar with both my academic successes and my failures, some I had never met before, and some were members of the Committee itself. I vowed to leave no stone unturned in my commitment to be reinstated into medical school.

But I knew that in the end it was my struggle alone. I took time to analyze my overall strengths and weaknesses to determine how those fit in with the study of medicine. Then I began outlining a strategy to improve my performance. I wanted to create a document that would convince the Committee and serve me as a guide if I was given a second chance.

In its final form, the document was thirty-two pages long, with eight separate sections. It was reviewed by sixteen professors and physicians affiliated with the medical school, some of whom had written personal letters of support. The document also included a letter from the learning strategist who had analyzed my learning style and concluded that I was likely to be successful.

In my next appearance before the Promotions Committee some four long weeks later, there were fewer questions. Since I had forwarded the document to each member a full week before the meeting, they had had the opportunity to review it, and it answered many of their previous questions. In addition, the time and effort that went into the preparation of the document demonstrated my commitment to continue toward a career in medicine. This was a very different meeting than the first, and I came away feeling positive.

By the end of the day of my appeal I received an email from the Committee reinstating me as a first-year student in the school of medicine. I was also approached by the Dean of Academic Affairs and asked if the school could give my document to all students who were to face meetings with the Promotions Committee. I was pleased to agree, in the hopes that it would help other students who found themselves in my situation.

Below you will find an abbreviated version of the document I submitted to the Indiana University School of Medicine Student Promotions Committee. While it probably is not necessary to go into the detail that I have in this document, any student in serious academic trouble should spend time at least thinking through all of these details, even if they don't write them down. However it is best if you write out your petition, so that you can study it carefully and anticipate questions. If you are willing to do that, there's a good chance that you'll succeed and that the Committee will make its own recommendations concerning the steps you will take to improve your performance. By the way, I graduated in May 2005. I encourage you to continue believing in yourself and your abilities. You can make it, too! Good luck and God bless.

Prognosis for Success

When I received notice to appear before the Committee for a second time, I had to take a long, hard look at my skills and limitations for the study and practice of medicine. I knew that I would have to assure them that my commitment was still very strong. Here's the inventory I came up with:

- Most of the study of medicine fits squarely within my area of strengths.

- In areas where I have been weak, further study will develop new skills.

- My desire, motivation, and my conviction that I will make a good doctor will help me recover from this setback.

- The experience of being called before the Committee in itself has taught me a great deal.

I didn't stop there but did further stock-taking. During my self-review, I thought carefully about the qualities that make a good medical student and concluded that, while I had many of those qualities, or I would not have been admitted to medical school, I also, like everyone else, had specific limitations. The Committee had especially asked me to consider whether I allowed myself enough time for study, whether I managed that time effectively, and whether I knew how to study. In looking at these areas, I put aside all excuses, dodges, or anything else that might keep me from being honest about my weaknesses. If you find yourself in a similar situation, I urge you to follow my course. When the chips are down, it's time to be real about who you are.

Look at any psychological or emotional quirks that might have weakened your performance. For example, for some, being away from home combined with the rigors of medical school can make you feel lonely, isolated, and without the solid support your family provided in the past. You may also have specific issues like the loss of a loved one, financial difficulties, physical ailments, or even a break-up with a close friend or spouse. But a word to the wise: Don't fake an excuse. The people on your committee are professors and physicians who have seen it all. They will know if you are being honest. Now for more details.

LEARNING STRATEGIES

I went to a learning strategist for assistance in evaluating my learning style. She had been with the medical school for more than twenty years helping students find ways to improve their academic performance. Here are some of the issues I was able to discover with her help:

My Strengths

We found that I had good qualities going for me, such as:

- Ability to create and follow a plan

- Ability to easily understand complex concepts and theories

- Ability to understand written material well

- Ability to work within a team framework

- Ability to work well independently

- Ability to make decisions about information in a logical/ analytical way

- Ability to work long periods of time to achieve a goal

- Ability to work in a steady, orderly way

- Record of past academic success

- Confidence in my abilities.

My Limitations

- Tendency to overlook details for the sake of concepts and theories

- Reticence to seek help or assistance when need is first identified

- Tendency to focus on one subject at a time to the detriment of other subjects.

Study Time

I told the professors that since I began my work towards medical school four years ago, I had consistently recorded the amount of time I spent studying, not including breaks or other interruptions. It turned out to be approximately seven hours per day. I slept five to six hours per weeknight, as had been my habit for the past several years. This schedule worked for me; however you will need to evaluate your own allotted time for study.

Study Management

My place of study was generally the library or the Daly Student Center, and, occasionally, home. I studied alone because interruptions and questions from colleagues easily interfered with my concentration.

Early in the school year, I studied mainly from class notes I had transcribed without making much use of supplemental texts. I enlisted only the aid of Netter's *Atlas* and Grant's *Dissector* and was unaware of Grey's *Anatomy* until the course director suggested it to me as we began preparation for my summer remediation. I focused my early medical studies almost exclusively on cell and molecular biology, since earlier diagnostic tests indicated that I might have trouble in this area. I passed this course, but I began the practice of "ping-ponging" that would continue throughout the year. Concentrating on one subject at a time, I ran into trouble with gross anatomy.

As the year progressed, I solicited the help of classmates, who suggested several techniques to aid my study sessions: They recommended that I:

- Always keep a copy of Stedman's *Medical Dictionary* at my side during study

- Use Board Review Series books

- Thoroughly rehearse packet learning objectives

- Use a white board.

During my first year, I employed these techniques in preparing for the immunology final and earned a passing score. I continued to use them in preparing for the second histology exam and saw similar positive results. For the last histology examination, I took the additional step of enlisting the help of a professor and I saw dramatic results: a score of 86.5 percent on an interim examination. But later, I slipped and failed the course.

I studied exclusively for the respiratory section of physiology and felt that I had mastered the material. Unfortunately, as the result of overconfidence, I failed to test my understanding with the professor. My mistake led to my score of 67.5 percent on the test. During that bad year, I continued to jump from course to course and to get disappointing results—first, in the bacteriology section of microbiology, and then in the GI/renal sections of physiology.

EMOTIONAL HURDLES

Speaking with my learning counselor, I could report no outside distractions that contributed to my poor academic performance, but I did have trouble making the adjustment to full-time study after a ten year absence from school. In my first semester, I didn't make that adjustment successfully, as indicated by my struggles in gross anatomy, which began when we reached the final section. I attended every class, sitting in the first row, and reviewed the clearly presented material immediately after class and again upon receipt of the class notes. During this section I attended lab consistently, and spent long nights working in the lab with a group of classmates. I studied over fall break, not leaving the library until closing time. My poor performance on that examination shocked me, because I had always experienced academic success consistent with my study efforts.

FINDING THE RIGHT TECHNIQUES

Under the guidance of my counselor, who had already had me do a Myers-Briggs Type Indicator test (MBTI) to aid in her analysis of my learning style, I identified the three to five areas that most harmed my academic performance. After identifying these areas, using the self-knowledge I had gained from personal analysis combined with feedback from professors and other students, I identified techniques and study aids that would strengthen each area. I took time to evaluate the techniques before deciding on the one or two that I thought would serve me best. While there is always some room for experimentation, don't take an entire semester to decide. Find what works and stay with it!

Here's what I came up with, with the help of the counselor:

1. **I had a tendency to overlook details for the sake of concepts and theories.**
   Theoretical courses such as immunology, physiology, and concepts of health and disease (CHD) came naturally to me. Gross anatomy and histology, because they involved greater scientific detail, caused me more trouble and required a detailed study plan that included:

   A. Using videotapes
      My learning style, I now understood, required that I see the study material repeatedly. Videotapes helped me because they could be paused and because they allowed repeated viewing of critical material. In the anatomy course, in fact, the department recommended a series of tapes—*The Video Atlas of Human Anatomy*—to help us review the intricate material.

B. *Using lab time more efficiently*

The learning strategist recommended that I use a color atlas with actual photographs of the cadavers *before* I went to lab to perform dissections. Seeing the material clearly beforehand made me feel more confident and knowledgeable when I faced the actual task.

C. *Using the Board Review Series during summer and the following fall*

In some courses, the textbooks themselves gave me a firm base for learning the material. In others, important areas were treated less completely in the texts than I needed. In those cases, I backed up my readings in the text with additional study of the Board Review Series books, which were of particular help to me in my study of biochemistry.

D. *Using Flash Cards*

In subjects in which memorization of key words and phrases is critical, I found flash cards useful. Through them, I was better able to recall specific details of a large body of information—details I might otherwise forget under the pressure of test situations. They helped me especially in immunology and in the virology section of microbiology to achieve good results.

2. **I had been reticent to seek help at the time I first realized that I needed it.**

I had always enjoyed academic success because I was able to work independently for long periods of time to achieve a goal. Now, as I learned from my setback, I realized that these strengths weren't adequate in themselves. I also had to know when I needed help, and to know it early enough for it to be effective. I found that many professors were happy to mentor me. At the same time, I found that I could make best use of their help by becoming an active partner in the mentoring relationship. To do that, I learned to:

A. *Develop a list of questions before my meeting with the professor.*

Writing down questions beforehand helped me to identify

areas of weakness. It also let me discover if I *needed* help. If I couldn't come up with an answer to a question by myself despite my best efforts at research, study, and reflection, I knew that I had to go to the professor for clarification. My visits weren't always in person. Most professors welcomed questions submitted via email.

B. *Meet individually with my professors.*
In classes where I felt weakest or most confused, I scheduled routine weekly meetings with each professor. During these meetings, we would go over questions not suitable to email, and discuss the current course material. Together, we would review the objectives of the section of study, and I would identify the areas that were causing me the most trouble.

C. *Enroll in individual summer study programs.*
In these summer programs, several of my professors generously developed study plans for me weekly. At the conclusion of each week's course of study, I met with them to discuss the material. Following the session, I was required to complete a test on the week's material. In some cases, the tests were developed from Board Review Series examinations in gross anatomy and biochemistry, while in others the professor drew up tests directly based on course material. Afterwards, we discussed the test results and evaluated my progress.

D. *Work in small, carefully selected study groups.*
I discovered that my former practice of always studying alone now worked less well for me than working with a small group of serious and focused students. Throughout the school year we met regularly and tested our understanding of the material by quizzing one another.

3. **I had always tended to focus on one subject at a time.**
Here, too, my old strength had become a handicap in medical school. Now, whether I liked it or not, I had to give constant attention to each subject. To achieve this, I briefly reviewed

all class and transcribed notes in order to reacquaint myself with the overall concepts presented in a particular lecture. I then reread the material for the purpose of outlining it and refining details. In a third reading, I pored over the lecture's finer points.

These, then, were the main elements of the document I prepared for the review board. As I began to implement them, I soon got results, particularly in gross anatomy, the subject in which I had gotten into trouble. Now, because I had learned to use my time more efficiently, and because I accepted the task of keeping up with *everything,* I was able to give to this course the time and focus it needed. I don't mean to suggest that everything I proposed to do worked, but little by little I was transforming myself from a marketing expert into a scientist and physician. What held me up through all this was my deep-seated determination to serve society as a doctor.

HOW TO PREPARE FOR A MEETING WITH
A STUDENT PROMOTION COMMITTEE

1. Self Analysis

Begin by taking a hard look at your academic strengths and weaknesses. Weaknesses can include anything—poor study habits, lack of knowledge in a certain area, psychological issues you must face and deal with, and so on.

Areas you may wish to analyze especially carefully are:

- Study management
- Test management
- Psychological issues

2. Strategies for Improving Your Performance

Once you have identified weaknesses that hurt your academic performance, you can find ways to get past them.

For example, if your problem is that you overlook details:

- Use videotapes
- Use lab time more efficiently
- Review with help of books from the Board Review Series
- Use flash cards.

If you have been reticent to seek help from professors:

- Develop a list of questions before meeting with professors.
- Schedule routine weekly meetings with each professor.
- Enroll in summer study programs with professors.
- Seek out and work in small, carefully selected study groups.

If your problem is that you have only focused on one subject at a time:

- Review all classes and transcribed notes upon receipt.
- Review first year's material before class.
- Maintain focus on all classes.
- With the advice and consent of your professors, draw up a summer study plan to strengthen your knowledge in areas where it is deficient.

CHAPTER 7

A Born Natural

*Robert Patterson's story is of a second career and of obstacles overcome;
Anthony N. Harris's story recounts a life that seemed destined for science and
medicine almost from the beginning.*

Let's face it: The road to medical school isn't easy. However, any journey is easier to endure when you maintain an underlying sensibility of fun and enjoyment. And to do that you must first be sure that you, rather than pressures imposed by the hopes of others, have determined the road on which you travel.

Since I can remember, I have always viewed problems as a challenge to my ability to derive a particularly unique solution. This of course, is my adult viewpoint: My mother remembers me as a toddler who, when confronted with the task of picking up my toys, would try to carry all of the toys together instead of taking a few at a time. This method may have made it take longer for me to move all the toys, but it worked, and success at such simple tasks prepped the canvas on which I would paint my philosophy of innovation towards the solutions of life's dilemmas.

As an adolescent, instead of always playing outside, I remained indoors to play with Lego building blocks. It was common for me to dismantle my Christmas toys in order to salvage the parts as materials for electronic creations of my own. Once, when I was eleven, I fashioned a portable, hand-held fan out of cardboard, batteries, an electric motor, and wood. The device was quite effective in combating Florida's summer heat, and my relatives and friends of the family marveled at it. Later, when I was in ninth grade, I discovered that the concept of hand-held personal fans had exploded into almost every convenience store in the nation. I was dismayed to see others profit from what I thought of as my invention, but at the same time I began to realize the market potential of my ideas.

Both my parents, Nathaniel and Cynthia, fostered my creativity by bringing home various pieces of junk that I was ecstatic to receive and incorporate into a new device. They also exposed me to experiences that further opened my vision of technology. We lived near Kennedy Space Center, and the launch of the space shuttle became a regular backyard spectacle for me and my community. Since my father was employed as a government auditor and frequently worked on projects at NASA, my family was able to visit the Space Center on "Family Days". This annual family event became one of the highlights of my adolescent years. I was awed by the complexity and magnitude of the technological advances that allowed men to step onto the moon, and before long, I was clamoring to become an astronaut.

Once I reached my teenage years and entered junior high, however, my focus shifted from the vastness of space to the finitely small world of micro and molecular biology. In seventh grade, I found myself in the engineering division of a company of science researchers, and my experience there was very positive. A few years later, when I entered the division of medicine and health in the same company, I first felt an ambition to become a physician. In research competitions, I received first and second place regional and state honors, and I was awarded a month-long summer internship in the local hospital. During the internship, I researched the effects of electromagnetic fields on living organisms. This research led to my interest in radiology.

Through all this, my ambitions to become an astronaut never quite faded, and they were rekindled when, in my junior year, I entered a program called NURTURE (NASA's Unique Residential

Training for Up-and-coming Replacement Engineers). The program gave 50 students from around the state the opportunity to travel to NASA once a month to learn more about the technical and biological advances of the space program.

As a result of my experience in science research and involvement with the NURTURE program, a group of other students from across the country and I were invited to participate in the launching of an experimental rocket designed to study the dynamics and composition of the various atmospheric layers. As a result of my work on this project, I was one of three student speakers at an international education summit called EURECA, which was held on the grounds of NASA's conference facilities.

In high school, I continued to conduct research in the division of medicine and health, again investigating the effects of electromagnetic fields on human tissue cultures. During my senior year, my research attempted to uncover possible links between genetic mutations in p53, a protein, and the occurrence of cancer.

I received a full scholarship to Florida Agricultural and Mechanical University (FAMU), and, soon after, an additional scholarship made possible through the generosity of Dr. George Rawls. From that second scholarship grew a relationship that would pave the remainder of my journey towards medical school.

My major at FAMU was biology pre-medicine, with a minor in chemistry. It certainly kept me busy. But I was also after leadership experience, and, with encouragement from my sister, Cynathia, ran for one of eight positions in the student senate. After a few weeks of intense campaigning, I was elected from a pool of 36 candidates to serve a two-year term as a freshman senate representative. My quick acclimation to the legislative climate of the senate allowed me to gain insight into the administrative procedures of both student-facilitated organizations and the university at large.

During my second year as a representative, I was appointed to serve as chair of two budget committees responsible for the allocation of more than $3.2 million to campus agencies and organizations. My sophomore year became my trial by fire, for aside from the extracurricular duties, I also carried a strictly science-based class load of 21 hours. Friends and co-workers told me that my expectations of keeping all this up were a little delusional, but I insisted that if I could survive and emerge undamaged, then I would be ready for the rigors of medical school.

By the end of my sophomore year I realized that success is a state of mind—it belongs to those confident that they will succeed. I won my second election during the spring semester to serve another two-year term in the senate. Elected to the position of senate president pro-tempore (vice president) in my junior year, I played an integral part in leading a march of more than 3,000 students to Florida's capitol building in reaction to the disenfranchisement of student voters during the 2000 Presidential Elections. The Reverend Jesse Jackson joined us in our efforts when I, and other student leaders from FAMU and Florida State University, met with Catherine Harris, who at the time was the Florida Secretary of State. Thoroughly dissatisfied by the unresponsiveness of the state government offices, including the Governor's, more than 1,500 students spent the night in the state capitol building.

When I was elected the thirty-first president of the Student Senate, I was able to structure the organization of the senate in a fashion I had been planning during my years of involvement. All in all, my four-year involvement within the FAMU student senate accorded me many valuable experiences—from developing a personal working relationship with our distinguished university president, Dr. F.S. Humphries, to greeting visiting celebrity entertainers, to hosting a question and answer session with former Attorney General Janet Reno.

I am convinced that participation in activities outside the classroom that benefit the environment, fellow students, or community, are as essential as academic events. Such involvement broadens our far-reaching effect as students, all the while enriching our lives and overall experiences in academia. When I entered medical school, however, things changed. Although I had intended to continue participating in student government throughout medical school, a wise promise made to Dr. Rawls placed those ambitions on hold.

I first stepped onto the campus of Indiana University School of Medicine after my freshman year of undergraduate college at FAMU.

That summer I spent almost two months in the department of pulmonology conducting research related to cancer detection. The experience offered me a first glimpse of Midwest life, and introduced me to a season I'd never really experienced. Odd as it may seem, the anticipation of a breezy, frigid winter added to the allure of life in Indiana.

After my second visit to IU School of Medicine in the summer following my junior year, I had firmly decided to attend IU. With the help of Dr. Rawls and letters of recommendation from other faculty members with whom I had become acquainted, my ambitions were met and I became the first person in my family to attend medical school.

Dr. Rawls, who serves as my mentor, advised me to focus on the classroom and to minimize my participation in student government during the first year of medical school. That decision paid off. I learned what was required to maintain success in meeting the rigorous educational demands of medical school. But then, once I had my first year's classes in balance, I resolved to participate in the medical student council.

During the spring of my first year, I interviewed for, and was appointed to, the dean's position of Organization of Student Representative (OSR). As IU School of Medicine representative to the Association of American Medical Colleges (AAMC), I traveled to annual national and regional meetings to discuss pertinent matters with other student representatives from across the country and relayed information back to my student constituency. In the fall of 2003, I vied for and was elected president of the class of 2006. I was the first African American at the IU School of Medicine to hold that distinction.

What lies ahead for me? In the summer before my third year of medical school I began course work for an MBA. You might wonder how the MBA ties in to medicine. Well, that's a whole new story. Recall when I spoke of the days when I used to sit at home designing and fashioning new gadgets and inventions? Those hobbies never left me. In fact, my passion for innovation has developed over the years into a path that parallels my journey into the world of medicine.

Recently, I have been drawn to the possibilities of entrepreneurship in the rapidly expanding domain of biotechnology. In this choice, the combination of my creativity and penchant for innovation, my goal of practicing radiological medicine, and my strides towards business ownership in technology has come full circle. It's my wish not only to remain knowledgeable about future medical advances in radiology, but also to stand at the forefront of those advances. I am currently conducting clinical research that explores new developments and possible applications of nuclear medicine. In several years, after I have graduated and practiced medicine in my self-owned medical group, I intend to use my research, creativity, and technical experience to develop new devices and procedures for radiology and other medical fields in general.

With God on my side and the near completion of my first U.S. patent, I am closer than ever towards making my dreams a reality. And, although my path may no longer lead me to explore the depths of space, the trek of an astronaut and my journey towards the practice of medicine still share a promising commonality: From this point on, there is nowhere to go but up.

CHAPTER 8

Grief Made Me a Doctor

Glenda Ramirez, Sophomore Medical Student

When Glenda Ramirez's father fell ill and died, she knew what she wanted to do with her life. Now, as a result of hard struggle, she is on her way to doing it.

I was born and reared in a small mining town in northern Mexico. I haven't always been interested in the study of medicine; in fact, my goal growing up was to be a concert pianist or music teacher, and I carried that ambition into high school. At that time, my brothers were attending the University of Notre Dame, from which they graduated with honors with degrees in chemical engineering. I had read and heard so much about this famous university that I too decided to apply, but at the time my family was in financial straits and could not afford the tuition, so I went to work as a secretary to help the family financially.

After the economy improved, my father insisted that I attend Notre Dame. I applied and was accepted. That's when I decided that music was not a practical career for me and chose to pursue a degree in economics. I was awarded my bachelor's degree in economics and thought that it would be relatively easy to find a first-rate job, but I was mistaken. I resigned myself to accepting any job I could get.

Unfortunately, my father became very ill, so I wasn't able to take any job. Instead, I was introduced to the world of medicine during my father's long hospital stay that started on December 21, 1988. He had been ill for a few days but no one imagined the gravity of the problem. I remember the evening when I took him to the ER. I felt helpless, and all the white coats, the medical equipment, the beeping sounds, and the smells of the hospital frightened me. Throughout my father's difficult and trying six weeks there, his spirits and energy gradually dwindled. As he lay dying, I was angry that I didn't know how to help ease his pain, much less cure him. He was more tranquil than I. He knew he was dying but expressed no fear because his loved ones surrounded him.

When I visited him shortly before his death, his eyes followed me wherever I moved. All he wished for me in life was happiness. At just this time, I saw my path. My interest in medicine had been sparked by my desire to understand my father's illness, and I wanted to care for, and ease the fears of people who were ill.

After my father's death, I heard there was an opening for a bilingual secretary at a doctor's office in Tucson, Arizona. I applied and got the job. Working for a busy bilingual general surgeon was a breathtaking opportunity. It let me see firsthand, the many roles a physician plays. My boss's practice wasn't confined to surgical cases; he provided family medicine as well. His patients were like family. Not only did he provide them with excellent medical care, he also inspired confidence, optimism, and faith.

Because of my business experience, I was able to perform my duties quickly and efficiently, allowing me spare time to work in the back office and to "shadow" the doctor. I watched him examine, listen to, operate on, and advise many patients. Initially, I was merely curious, but with the passing of time, I became mesmerized by the doctor's patience, respect, and compassion for his patients. I witnessed many a previously ill patient's return for a change of dressing with a big smile. They were glad for the opportunity to see him. I saw the patients' affection for him time and again—an elderly woman would bring a cake for the doctor, or an old man would bring a hand-carved ornament, all in appreciation for being healed or relieved of pain. The human spirit I saw in the doctor's relationship with his patients overwhelmed me.

I realized then and there that I would pursue a career in medicine no matter how long it would take. I admired the doctor's ability to communicate with many patients in both Spanish and English. I felt fortunate that I was bilingual and had developed a good knowledge of medical terminology in both languages. I dreamed of someday being able to emulate this excellent physician. Soon therafter, I became his medical assistant and loved it.

The doctor inspired and encouraged me to pursue a medical career. So whenever I had the opportunity (I worked full time), I took the prerequisite courses for medical school at the University of Arizona. The road to my goal was long and bumpy, but I was determined to succeed. I owe my tenacity to my beloved father. I also owe much to God and my country and wish to give back as much as I can.

Now, as I near the end of my first grueling semester of medical school, I am sleep-deprived and cannot function without drinking a lot of coffee. I know what a healthy diet is, but mine consists mostly of peanut butter sandwiches and pizza. I am full of anxieties: *Will I get to Dr. Harris's biochemistry lectures on time? I have nightmares in which Dr. Shew comes over to my dissecting table to discover that I forgot everything I've learned in anatomy. Will I learn the genetic code so I can stop pestering Dr. Wek with all my questions in cellular and molecular biology?.* On top of these sources of anxiety, immunology, concepts of health and disease, introduction to clinical medicine, and evidence-based medicine provide me with abundant, heavy reading material just in case I get bored in my spare time! I have piles of lectures to review and have forgotten what it means to have a social life. In spite of all of this, I could not be happier! I would not trade this for anything in the world!

CHAPTER 9

Against All Odds

Antoinette Austin-Glass, M.D., Anesthesiologist

Some medical students know early that they were meant to be doctors and move directly to their goal. Others, equally clear about career choice, must struggle against obstacles that for others would be insurmountable. Antoinette Austin-Glass was discouraged by counselors from pursuing a medical career. They told her that as a Black woman, she didn't have a chance. But she never lost faith that she could realize her dream. It wasn't easy. Dr. Austin-Glass was sometimes detoured by bad advice, by her responsibilities to her husband and child, and by academic setbacks, but her eyes were always on the prize.

I do not ask to walk smooth paths nor bear an easy load.
I pray for strength and fortitude to climb the rock-strewn
    road.
Give me such courage and I can scale the hardest peaks
    alone,
And transform every stumbling block into a steppingstone.

—Gail Brook Burket

When I was five years old, my mother suffered an accident on the job that left her without the full use of her left leg. A few weeks after the accident, my father and a nurse devised a plan to sneak me into the hospital to see her. Stepping into the hospital was so charged with wonder and curiosity! I saw all the people working to help my mother and the other patients to get better, and I decided right then that I wanted to be just like them. When my mother finally recovered and came back home, I announced to the family that I planned to become a doctor when I grew up.

My mother struggled long and hard to regain a normal life. She was faced with the harsh reality that employers did not want to hire handicapped people. Many told her to give up and go on welfare or disability; after all, she had a legitimate reason to do so. Instead, she fought for, and won back her original job, where she had been a model employee and worked there until her retirement. My mother's struggle to rise in the face of adversity and to achieve against all odds taught me the importance of self-respect and belief in myself even if no one else did, and of knowing that I could do anything I wanted if I set my mind to it.

During my junior year of high school, I sought advice from a high school counselor about how to make my dream a reality. Unfortunately, she did not share my vision and strongly advised me against my choice of becoming a doctor. I suppose she was focused on the facts that I came from a divorced home, was a product of an inner city school system, and, if that weren't enough, was the third child of a physically disabled mother who never finished high school. She told me, "You are Black, female, and smart. You should seriously think about engineering because you don't have much of a chance of becoming a doctor." From a statistical standpoint she was probably right, but statistics do not provide a formula for calculating the impact of a loving, God-fearing mother who may not have been formally educated, but had wisdom that cannot be learned in school.

I knew that in order to go to school I would need financial aid, so I accepted a full engineering scholarship to Kentucky State University. I vowed that engineering would be the road I would take, but medicine would be my final destination. I soon learned that the road would have many detours and roadblocks.

After I completed a successful year at Kentucky State University, I transferred to Purdue University in order to be closer to home. In 1982, I graduated with a degree in industrial management, with a focus in engineering. My new career led me to a position at AT&T where my work was cut out for me. I was the only Black female and was assigned an unproven territory—the marketing of phone services to other Black women. I was able to exceed my objective and received several awards recognizing my sales and marketing achievements. After five years, I was offered an opportunity to put my technical, marketing, and interpersonal skills to use in product development with Indiana Bell/Ameritech. I even earned a master's degree in business administration while working full time. Yet, despite my successes, eventually I had to face the fact that I was not fulfilled.

For many years, I had been a volunteer for the Gennerset Free Clinic, which provided free medical services for the poor and homeless. I donated my evenings and weekends despite my demanding schedule, because I felt I was making a lasting difference. In my volunteer work, I learned firsthand about the skills and compassion it took to be a good physician. I began to realize that it was time to make a change. I was ready to be true to my original dream of becoming a physician, though I knew that it would involve serious new challenges. I was now a wife and mother and would need to find a balance between my medical studies and my responsibilities to my family.

Medical school is difficult. I found myself struggling to manage the time demands of my two lives. That struggle resulted in my failing physiology. While at first I was devastated, I was able to take this setback as a challenge. I was not discouraged, and I successfully completed my physiology requirement during remediation.

During my second year, my husband learned that his father was dying of renal failure as a result of diabetes and hypertension. When he was told that a kidney transplant could save his father's life, he did not hesitate to volunteer as a donor. After he tested as a good match, we traveled to Illinois for the transplant surgery. Following the surgery, my husband had some complications that delayed his recovery and we found ourselves making several trips to Chicago for further treatment.

While I tried to remain focused on my studies, my concern for my family was too overwhelming. I chose to focus my attention on my family and took a leave of absence. While some may have given up at this point, I was firm in my conviction that medicine was where I was supposed to be. Once my husband was given a clean bill of health, I returned to medical school and successfully completed my second and third years.

My next challenge was to choose a specialty. I wrestled hard with this problem, but in the end I chose anesthesiology. I liked the notion of working in an operating room setting, and I also knew that an anesthesiologist needed a clear understanding of the body's physiology. Finally, an anesthesiologist must do a lot of problem solving, sometimes on the spot. It all seemed to fit me to a T.

During my surgery clerkship, I had enjoyed the behind-the-scene hustle and bustle, and was especially intrigued by the drugs and equipment that are part of the process. Now, as I entered the actuality, I was hooked! Being part of a team, coordinating with the surgeons, and performing the hands-on procedures left me with a sense of accomplishment. I eagerly returned each day anticipating the challenges each new case would bring. I am now looking for a program in which my skills as an anesthesiologist will continue to grow.

The process of picking myself up and dusting myself off has enriched my life and deepened my resolve to become a physician. The most rewarding part of this whole experience is that by not giving up I have passed on to my daughters, the message given to me by my mother—that the only difference between a stumbling block and a stepping-stone is perspective.

CHAPTER 10

Getting Past Test Anxiety

Sean Eugene Gardner, M.D., Anesthesiologist

I was born and reared in Terre Haute, Indiana, a small town west of Indianapolis on US 70. I look back at the town as a drab place on the way to somewhere else. When I was growing up, no one stressed academics, and college did not often come up in conversation. My contemporaries were making no plans for a future and I lived as they did.

I am not trying to create a picture of "life in the hood" such as you see on popular TV cop shows. Although many people around me fit that lifestyle, my family tried to keep me away from them. Still, my environment didn't encourage me to envision myself in a real career. Instead, throughout my growing up years there was a pervasive absence of expectation. Neither my mother, aunts and uncles, nor my cousins were greatly concerned with school performance; rather, everyone's energies were directed to managing their individual and family survival. As a Black boy in a mediocre town, I saw where I was headed: maybe to working at a job that didn't pay well, and having an obligation for child support. Or maybe it would be drugs, violence, and prison.

As a result of family hardships, my view of the world was limited and unsure. I was uprooted a few times and felt "out of sync" each time I started at a new school. Then, at a happy point during these years, I went to Indianapolis to live with my dad. There, I found stability. I had become a cynic, and believed I could trust no-one but myself. This new environment brought a new perspective.

I determined to start afresh at Broad Ripple High School and to make academics and athletics my prime priorities. Whether I was led by intuition or divine guidance, the combination of these two activities would become my keys to success. Personally, I think it was divine guidance.

I became interested in medicine initially because it related to sports and physical performance. My drive to win in football fueled this interest. My goal was to develop muscle, strength, and endurance. As a practical matter, I read and learned about my body. I gave up the fun that I saw my friends enjoying because I was dedicated to my football obligations. I passed up most of the usual high school events in favor of study to ensure that I could play football. I did well at Broad Ripple High School because of football. And football helped me move on to the next step: enrollment in college.

I am the first in my immediate family to earn a college degree. When I arrived on the campus of the small, private university to which I had been accepted, I was inexperienced socially, unprepared academically, and out of my league financially. Most of the other students had had top-notch educations provided by parents who were industry leaders and professionals, and my university was alma mater to consecutive generations of prominent citizens. My classmates were following footsteps along a well-worn path. I, on the other hand, was traveling new ground. I had only attitude and determination to level the playing field. Throughout undergraduate school, my focus was on achieving. Failure was not an option.

Again, I have to credit football for driving me along my path. My university recruited me with an academic scholarship. Coaches wanted a hard-playing athlete, but it also didn't hurt the university that I could be counted toward their minority quota. It was a two-way street. I made outstanding achievements on the field. I was named team captain and was recognized as MVP, as Offensive Player of the Year, and for other achievements on the field.

Yet, although I was a football star, I barely rated average in academics. When I took the MCAT in my junior year I scored poorly, and I scored no better when I took the exam the second time. I graduated with a 2.7 GPA. I had counted on the university's reputation (and my good intentions) to launch me into medical school, so I was crushed to acknowledge that my MCAT score would not get me there. I felt a deep sense of loss. My dad was encouraging, reminding me that I could always take the test again, but that was of little consolation.

Fortunately, my dad is resourceful. He knew Dr. Rawls and arranged for me to meet with him. In 1995, Dr. Rawls was Assistant Dean of Student Affairs at Indiana University School of Medicine when I met him. He had reviewed my case and naturally noticed my low MCAT scores. I acknowledged to him that I had done poorly on most tests. He listened to me describe the long hours I spent in preparing for each. I told him truthfully that I consistently studied longer than my classmates and that I knew the material better than most. I also mentioned the sense of doom that bubbled up from my gut each time I sat before an answer sheet with a No. 2 pencil and my feeling of defeat when the test scores came back.

Dr. Rawls made a simple statement. I was not a competitive applicant because of my poor test taking. He helped me understand that I could commit an entire textbook to memory, but would probably never test any higher if I didn't learn to take tests. This was a different way to understand my poor performance.

Dr. Rawls was at the same time sympathetic and no-nonsense. He recommended two steps. He advised that I get evaluated psychologically, and told me that my emotional and physical distress at test taking time, were symptoms of a real disorder. With an accurate diagnosis we would find out how to overcome it. I felt relieved. This problem was not a matter of intelligence or aptitude.

As to my second step, Dr. Rawls brought my attention to a Masters of Science in Medical Science (MSMS) program he was creating for students like me, who had aptitude and a willing heart but a deficient toolbox of skills. I became one of the first apprentices of the program.

It was during the two years of the MSMS program that I underwent several diagnostic tests conducted by learning specialists and was found to have "severe testing anxiety." This symptom explained my miserable test scores at the secondary school and college levels. More importantly, it explained the toll that poor test taking had been taking on me emotionally. I learned techniques for managing anxiety before and during test taking which began to show results. The accepted clinical diagnosis, "severe testing anxiety," even bought me longer test-taking time. I finished the two year program with a GPA of 3.7; but more importantly, I was able to bring my MCAT score up to the medical school's entry requirement. Were it not for Dr. Rawls and his accurate assessment of my problem (and my potential), I would not be enjoying my second year of residency in anesthesiology today!

Indiana University School of Medicine was another chapter in my chronicle of challenges. I can summarize it as a test of endurance. I still had to study three times harder and longer than the next guy, but I had learned some helpful study techniques in the MSMS program.

One of these was the matrix for group study. There was every reason for African-American students to join forces to tackle the volumes of material that *had* to be learned. The few of us there soon learned to rely upon one another in order to cover all the bases and fill in where another was deficient. Instead of feeling myself alone in my studies, I now found myself part of a supportive community of brothers and sisters.

I was also nurtured by a cadre of psychology professionals who taught me to assess each new situation and manage it successfully. I felt comfortable in this positive environment, even at testing time, and I excelled. I was accorded respect as a colleague while being encouraged to exercise my knowledge. I believe that a person is strengthened through challenge, and I certainly encountered several in the course of my medical education. Perhaps I would have achieved less than my genuine best if the road had been easier.

Part III

BEING A DOCTOR

CHAPTER 11

Internship and Residency

"The practice of medicine is an art based on science."
—*William Osler, Canadian Physician,*
also referred to as the Father of Medicine

These are the years of training when, as you are given progressively more responsibility, you learn to apply the principles you learned in medical school. You move up from the student's short coat to the doctor's long one. Your new experiences may also add to, or even alter, what you learned in medical school.

Because the paths open to a new doctor are so many, I can't provide a complete map of them here. Each specialty will present its own particular features, but in this and the following chapter, I will provide typical examples of experiences that may await you.

I will never forget my first day at Philadelphia General Hospital. I was covering psychiatry and was called to admit a middle-aged Black man diagnosed with schizophrenia. We discussed his family and work, and he seemed perfectly normal to me. After a pleasant interview, I wondered why he was being admitted. As I left him and wished him a good day, he exclaimed, "You know I'm Jesus Christ, don't you?" I had missed the diagnosis completely.

My next rotation was general surgery. Inside Philadelphia General in 1952-1953, peptic ulcers bled, inflamed colons burst, aneurysms ruptured, gallbladders became gangrenous, and hernias remained entrapped. Time off was rare. In fact, I had only two nights off a week. We interns lived, ate, and slept at the hospital while the outside world went on at a different, slower pace. Meanwhile at home, my wife's uterine waters broke prematurely, and our firstborn child, Yvonne, was born. I didn't know it for two days. Such was the life of an intern.

Besides, I was making $54 a month. I hadn't been as smart as Hans Geisler, a fellow intern. He had had the foresight to sign up for the Army while he was a senior in college, and they were helping him through medical school. He was commissioned a first lieutenant when he began his internship at Philadelphia General and was receiving approximately $400 a month. At the end of the internship, he was commissioned a captain. Oh well, so much for my foresight.

You make decisions and you live with them. Do not live in yesteryear. Live in "day-tight" compartments as suggested by William Osler, one of the great pioneers of modern medicine. Yesterday is truly yesterday. You can learn from it but you can never recapture it or correct its mistakes. Live today and prepare and look forward to tomorrow but do not worry about tomorrow.

The residency years are tiring and difficult, but here is where the young physician truly learns his specialty. My roommate, LaSalle Leffall, in later years was asked at a seminar what it took to be a good physician. In reply, he quoted Osler: "I will tell you what it takes. In fact, I will spell it for you—W-O-R-K." There is no substitute. What drives the work is a passion to learn, and the compassion to treat and assist those who are ill and come under your care. You must cure where you can, and relieve suffering and pain where you cannot.

The resident must continue to read the medical literature—not only the texts but also the current research that is published in journals. Reading must be a lifetime commitment. Remember, one of the competencies you developed in medical school was a hunger for life-long learning. This means, "until death do us part."

In the final year as chief resident, the physician learns in greater detail how to do procedures and interpret laboratory results as they relate to the specific patient. These activities mean long hours, missed meals, and still less sleep than before. Indeed, the life of a chief resident has become so demanding that current legislation is addressing the problem of overwork among interns and residents.

As of July 1, 2003, legislation went into effect that will have a great impact on all medical students, residents, and attending physicians in academic programs. First, there will be a mandatory limit on the number of hours that students and residents are allowed to work: eighty hours per week. Previously, the number of hours was unrestricted and many young doctors were relegated to caring for patients for days at a time without even leaving the hospital. These older requirements created frazzled, sleep-deprived students and residents who were forced to make medical decisions under extreme circumstances, causing poor patient care and outcomes. The new rules will allow more manageable lifestyles with predictable hours.

While this reform was long needed, it no doubt put greater pressure on attending physicians. They had become used to a regular and predictable schedule, thanks to the round-the-clock work of their juniors. In the old days, they sometimes made themselves unavailable on their ordinary call time, because, again, they could trust interns to take care of the patients. This is just one of the facts that you must consider when you choose whether to go into hospital-based or academic medical fields.

As the final year ends, new decisions await you. Will you practice solo or in a group, in an academic or managed-care environment? Solo practice works best in small towns. In large cities, it is more difficult to establish solo practice because most large cities have been infiltrated by managed care organizations that limit the number of physicians who can participate in their plans. Some state legislatures have established the concept of "any willing provider," which permits any practicing physician to participate in any managed care plan as long as the provider adheres to the established rules of the plan and accepts its payment schedule. This arrangement permits a patient who joins an HMO to keep his physician.

A physician who joins a group or works for an HMO or a hospital would be wise to have his or her contract reviewed by a competent attorney who specializes in this area. I knew a young physician who was terminated after one year as an employee of a hospital because she did not produce an income for the hospital that was comparable to her salary. Unfortunately, her contract contained a non-competing clause that prevented her from working or establishing a practice in the area for several years. She finally had to relocate and start anew. Meanwhile, her payments on student loans were due, along with other expenses for automobile costs and other necessities.

If you plan to enter solo practice, you would be prudent to plan in advance how to keep overhead as low as possible. The young physician might want to keep in mind this Chinese proverb: "A doctor's character should be square; his knowledge round; his gallbladder large [a sign of bravery]; and his heart small [a sign of carefulness]." Anyway, it is now time to "hang up the shingle" unless you plan further specialized studies.

PRIVATE OR GROUP PRACTICE

Just as in any job or profession, you want to watch for opportunities. Perhaps an older doctor is closing his office and wants to sell his practice or bring in a younger associate. Such a situation has several advantages. The practice is established, sparing you the ordeal of building a new one from the ground. Such opportunities turn up in any specialty, including family practice. If choices are available to you, you'll want to consider location, schools for the children, size of the community, availability of sports and cultural events, nearness of family, hospital facilities, among other criteria.

Having to start a practice from scratch has obvious disadvantages, especially for the minority physician whose practice is often limited primarily to patients of his own ethnicity. I knew a Black surgeon who had to move to three different cities in five years because he did not have the necessary volume of potential patients to serve.

As I've mentioned, it may be more difficult to establish an independent practice in larger cities. There, physicians of every specialty are already available. More importantly, there will have been an influx of managed care insurance companies (HMOs). Many HMOs restrict the number of physicians in each specialty. They may require that the physician be paid by "capitation," meaning that the physician is given a fixed sum of money for each patient cared for, regardless of the number or type of services the physician delivers. If you are not accepted into a managed care physician's group, you do not have access to the patients whom the HMO serves, and this may drastically restrict the growth of your practice. The good news is that, increasingly, states are passing "any willing provider" laws.

There are other pitfalls to look out for besides capitation. In many hospitals in large cities an established member of the staff must recommend the "new" doctor. If you did not do your training in the same city, or if you don't have contacts there, such a recommendation will be hard to get.

You can see why it's important for you to check the requirements for gaining privileges at a specific hospital before moving to a city and then discovering that the hospital isn't admitting new physicians to its staff or that you need recommendations you can't get. Remember that the recommending physician must be of the same specialty and may not wish to open his practice to competition for patients.

I remember seeking a place to practice and being warned that I should check to see if surgeons in Indianapolis would "accept" me. "How dare they not accept me?" I thought. "After all, I am a doctor and a surgeon. I have worked my butt off to obtain my training." I discovered that this wasn't enough. Yes, one must be trained. Yes, one must be board-eligible and eventually board-certified. However, the staff you want to join must also need someone with your specialty, and you must have a record of compatibility. In my case, two surgeons in Indianapolis who had not met me accepted letters from my chief. I was lucky enough to have an acquaintance that put me in contact with them.

Once you are on the job as a "new" physician, you may find yourself intimidated by the physicians who refer patients to you. I remember the first patient referred to me when I entered practice, a man with a fractured hip. I had rotated on orthopedics, but at that point I did not consider myself competent to "nail" a hip. "You mean you can't 'nail' a hip?" the older doctor asked me. He did not refer another case to me for more than a year.

Another physician referred an umbilical hernia patient to me. On further exam, I discovered that the primary problem was the presence of a huge fibroid tumor of the uterus. I asked the referring doctor if it was all right to ask a gynecologist colleague to perform a hysterectomy and then I would repair the hernia at the same operation. "You mean I refer you a case and you plan to have someone else do a procedure on her?" I did not hear from him again.

In another case, I was called to see "this nice little old lady" who had a bad leg. The referring doctor had been treating her for over a week, and in fact he had gone to her home daily. "I'm sure you can save her leg," he told me. "She is a sweet lady." However, when I saw her, her leg was black and obviously she urgently needed an amputation. In fact, the patient had a critical infection of the blood stream, with a low blood pressure. Although, when I explained this to the referring doctor, he was very unhappy, I went ahead, doing what I knew I had to do.

I placed a tourniquet above the dead lower leg, gave her massive doses of antibiotics and fluid for twenty-four hours, and then explained to her and her family why an amputation was necessary. They consented and I performed the surgery. Fortunately, the patient survived. But I never heard from this doctor again.

Fortunately, most of my referring doctors were excellent physicians and cared for their patients with compassion, integrity, and excellence. In addition, they would come to my rescue. I will never forget the second patient referred to me. She had gallstones and needed her gallbladder removed. I reviewed her chart and went in to her room and introduced myself. "Son, are you the surgeon my doctor sent in here to operate on me?" she asked. "I would never let a little jitterbug like you wearing a zoot suit operate on me. I'll talk to my doctor tomorrow." I was devastated. When I went home, I told Lula, my wife, that I was a failure and did not think I could succeed. "What happened?" she asked. When I told her that the patient said I was a jitterbug, Lu laughed so hard that she literally fell to the floor. "You, a jitterbug!" She exclaimed. " Never." I did not laugh. I was serious. *How was I going to support Lu and my three daughters?*

I called the referring doctor and explained to him my plight. "Don't worry," he said. "Let me see her first thing in the morning.

Then you go in later during the day." I don't know what he said to her, but when I returned, she was very pleasant, and she accepted me as her surgeon. She became a dear friend and referred many patients to me.

In the "good old days," I was always amazed how strong the patient-doctor relationship was between the referring family doctor and his patients. The physician was virtually a member of the family. He made house calls. He spent as much time as necessary talking to the patient and her family. Unfortunately, with managed care, the physician, working for a hospital or another group, has less control over the quality of attention he provides, and the doctor-patient relationship has deteriorated. Generally, the doctor has less time to give to the patient. In addition, many patients these days get their care in an emergency room rather than from a family doctor. The relationship is damaged further by the readiness of patients to file malpractice claims. Gone are the "good old days."

Black physicians may face problems particular to them. Often the physician and his patients attend the same church and are in the same social group. Under the circumstances, the patient may know the physician's wife. In such cases, the patient may worry: "Will he tell his wife about my condition?" Or, "He knows me socially and I do not want him to examine my breasts or do a pelvic on me." These are legitimate issues and the physician must understand them and work with them. Having his nurse in the examining room often helps solve the problem, but if the patient doesn't already know the nurse, she still may feel uncomfortable. The choice must be the patient's, but the fact that some women don't wish a male doctor to give the physical exam will limit the number of patients in one's practice. (And of course, this same pattern can develop when the patient is male and the doctor female.)

Another problem is that White patients may not like the idea having a Black doctor operate on them or a loved one. "He can prescribe medications. He can give me immunizations, but *operate?* I don't know about that." In my first year in practice, I was called to the emergency room of a hospital to see a very ill man. I examined him, ordered appropriate X-rays and laboratory work, and spent hours with him. When I indicated that he had a bowel obstruction and needed surgery, he sat up in bed, handed me a card, and said, "Did you say surgery? If I need surgery, call this White doctor to operate on me." And, of course, that was his privilege. I maintain that the patient must have the right to choose his provider. However, it was embarrassing for me. Moreover, I had spent hours with him. And, of course, his insurance pays only one surgeon. But he did well; therefore everything went well. For me, it was just a question of not letting my ego get involved.

The Business of Medicine

It must also be remembered that the practice of medicine is a business. With so much time, money and effort invested, the physician needs to handle money wisely when he or she is establishing the practice and thereafter. The goal is to keep the overhead below fifty percent of gross income. If you as a new physician are an independent, solo practitioner, you should locate in an area that will be readily accessible to your patients, and provides adequate free parking. The location should be also easily reached by bus and taxi. Staffing should be adequate but not excessive. Add staff members as needed.

The receptionist is very important. She is the initial contact at your office. Interview her well and instruct her that she must always be polite, sympathetic, and helpful to the patient and his family. Require good recommendations and, ideally, experience in running an office. You need to trust her common sense when the unexpected occurs, as it will.

The receptionist will also be the business manager until your practice grows to the point that you need an independent manager. Your receptionist needs skills in typing and in using a computer and other office machines. She also needs to be able to file and fill out insurance forms, unless you have an independent manager. Oftentimes, the receptionist becomes the business manager over the years because she understands the management of the office and your preferences.

A second important employee is a nurse or helper with the patients. Again, you'll wish to hire someone with common sense and compassion. This person should learn the basic skills in managing patients as she progresses in responsibility. Whenever you examine a patient of the opposite sex the nurse or helper should get the patient ready for your examination and be in the examining room when the examination takes place. This will help avoid accusations of inappropriate behavior.

For example, some patients don't understand that the physician must observe the differences in size and texture of both breasts, palpate the breasts for tumors, cup the breasts in his hands to detect a dimpling of tissue, and squeeze the nipples to check for bleeding or discharge. The presence of the helper assuages any apprehensions of the patient and protects the physician if there are accusations of abuse.

While a business manager may do the billing, or even if the billing is contracted out, the physician herself must oversee coding, billing and insurance procedures. I have known offices in which insurance forms were never submitted or were six months behind. These deficiencies should not be tolerated. Either the employee must be current in her work or, if need be, it should be contracted out. Obviously, the physician must periodically review the business of his office. If he is too busy, he needs an associate or should curtail his practice. But he must be the CEO of his office, be able to delegate duties, and be well aware of what is transpiring in his business.

Keeping Abreast of New Medical Discoveries

Needless to say, the physician must keep abreast of advances in medicine. The drug salesman, who has his own agenda, *cannot* be the only source of information. The physician should keep up with current knowledge by attending seminars, grand rounds, and other accredited CMEs (Continuing Medical Courses) as defined by the American Medical Association.

While the textbook is still a good source of basic information, you will need to subscribe to and read current journals in your specialty. While I was on the Indiana Medical Licensure Board, I often debated with other members, urging that physicians be required to accumulate a certain number of CME hours. The counterargument was that "you could lead a horse to water but you could not make him drink." While that is true, at least the horse has access to water. Fortunately, one of the competencies being emphasized at many medical schools now is "lifelong learning." It goes without saying that keeping up with one's field should be a part of the psyche of the student and, later, of the physician. For excellent information on courses available to you, see *www.intconf.com*.

How Am I Doing?

A doctor, no matter how competent, is not God. Patients may come out of treatment with complications, or even die. A good physician will want to know his numbers on these matters. Often the hospital itself provides this information, and you need to review it periodically. If your incidence of morbidity and mortality are subpar, you need to improve your techniques. For example, if a surgeon's infection rate for hernia repair is twice that of the accepted rate, he should review his technique of scrubbing both the patient and himself, and also review his sterile surgical technique.

In the office, you can evaluate outcomes by reviewing the success or failure of a given treatment or the number of return visits required to obtain a desired result. Before computers came into common use, some physicians used a coding process so that charts could be pulled and reviewed. Now, with computer programs, this process is less cumbersome. The objective of reviewing your work is to insure that the patient is receiving the best possible care. There is no higher satisfaction than a good patient-doctor relationship in which you feel confident that you have delivered the best of care in terms of competency and compassion, and that your efforts are appreciated by the patient and his family.

In a Nutshell

- Prepare yourself to become a competent physician.

- Select a city or town where you are needed and can give good service.

- Select a city or town where you and your family will enjoy living.

- Select a city or town where you can obtain hospital privileges easily.

- Decide carefully whether to be a solo practitioner, to join a group, or to be an employee of a clinic, hospital or HMO.

- Before signing a contract, seek advice from an attorney who specializes in physician employment.

- Always do what is in the best interest of the patient.

- Be kind, compassionate, and practice the best medicine you can.

- Always have an employee present when examining a patient of the opposite sex.

- Remember that the practice of medicine is an art.

- Be a lifelong learner and keep abreast of medical knowledge in your specialty.

- Remember that the running of an office is a business and that you are the CEO.

- Strive to keep the expense ratio at fifty percent or lower.

- Seek good employees, if you are solo, treat them well and provide adequate benefits.

- Become well rounded and contribute to the community.

- Do not neglect yourself or your family.

- Take vacations and enjoy hobbies.

CHAPTER 12

Academic Medicine

Academic medicine is very rewarding. I enjoyed immensely the five years I spent as an assistant dean and instructor at Indiana University School of Medicine, interacting with energetic, brilliant, innovative students. For many doctors, a lifelong career in teaching is the epitome of satisfaction. If you are inclined toward that kind of satisfaction, you may want to do your residency at a teaching institution well known in your anticipated area of specialty. Not only will the training be of the best quality, but a good recommendation from a well-known chief or colleague at your teaching institution will carry special weight when you apply for a position at any other institution. If you are a non-Caucasian, you can have special advantage, since minority medical academicians are in great demand. Less than two percent of medical faculties are African American.

The basic requirement is to become an exceptional physician or/and researcher. How does one become this person? Again I quote my friend, LaSalle Leffall, who often quotes the legendary Dr. William Osler: "I will tell you how to become an outstanding physician. In fact I will spell it for you: W-O-R-K."

This means sacrifice in time, because medical teaching is virtually a full-time job. You will have to review the literature with a particularly sharp eye for detail, and you will also have to convey your knowledge in a precise manner. As a medical academic, you will have to write grants and papers. Participating on administrative committees like admissions or promotion may not contribute very much in your quest for tenure or for advancement/promotion to full professor, but taking on the responsibility of selecting and teaching future physicians is a clear sign of dedication to the profession.

When I think of those who sacrificed to teach my classmates and me, I brim with thankfulness and admiration. Drs. Lester Henry, J. B. Johnson, Montague Cobb, Charles Drew, Burke Syphax, Ruth Moore, and Moses Young are but a few of the dedicated teachers who taught us at Howard University School of Medicine.

Recently, Michael Whitcomb, editor of the journal, *Academic Medicine*, in an article called, "Putting the School Back into Medical School," pointed out the importance of direct contact between professors and medical students. Robert D. Watson, M.D., senior associate dean at the University of Florida College of Medicine, also writing in *Academic Medicine*, has noted the unfortunate fact that although medical schools were once devoted to educating medical students, many evolved into Academic Medical Centers (AMCs) that place more emphasis on research than on educating future doctors. Dr. Watson reminds us that medical schools "have the mission of selecting and educating the next generation of physicians responsible for the care of the public."

In response to the concern that the medical schools place too little emphasis on the key importance of teaching, Drs. Cooke, Irby and Debas at the University of California, San Francisco (UCSF) report the development of an Academy of Medical Educators in their institution to encourage excellence in teaching, to support teachers of medicine and to promote curricular innovation. Three percent of the faculty at UCSF belong to the Academy. A similar academy has been established at Harvard Medical School to renew the emphasis on education, as reported by Dr. George E. Thibault in a 2003 issue of *Academic Medicine*.

The pattern of not encouraging students toward a teaching career has recently begun to change. Dr. Craig Brater, dean at Indiana University School of Medicine (IUSM), noted that a few years ago there was only one doctor with a Ph.D. in education at IUSM. He sought to hire more educators to instruct the residents on how to teach, since residents did a large share of the education of students and lower level residents at the school. Dr. Charles Hatem of Harvard reports that recently professionalism—that is, the student's dedication not merely to his own career but to the profession at large—has been emphasized as a core competency by the Accreditation Council for Graduate Medical Education (ACGME). Dr. Hatem notes that two complementary teaching initiatives promote professionalism: a resident-as-teacher program and improved bedside teaching. The refinement of residents' teaching skills helps to emphasize caring as a fundamental element of professionalism.

These shifts in emphasis make this an especially exciting time in medical education. So also does the explosion and expansion of knowledge. The human genome has been mapped, and genetic causes of diseases, such as sickle cell anemia and certain cancers, have been identified. The optimism generated by this rapid expansion of knowledge has predicted that there soon will be limited need for surgeons except in cases of trauma or transplantation. Naturally, it will be academic physicians who will expand, teach, and use this knowledge. Who knows? As one of many young people considering a career in medicine, you may be one of the forerunners in this endeavor. Why not seize the opportunity?

In a Nutshell

- Prepare yourself to be a good doctor.

- Choose the best possible school for your residency and for your fellowship in a specialty.

- Work diligently to learn what you need to know, understand it, and be able to apply it clinically and in research.

- Learn to teach, and aspire to be awarded the "Best Teacher" award given annually by most medical schools on the recommendation of students.

- Learn to write grant requests.

- Learn to write and contribute to medical literature.

- Live in such a manner that you are an inspiration to students and residents and enjoy the respect of your faculty colleagues.

- Make teaching your primary mission and your primary contribution to your community.

- Maybe the most important of your obligations is to remember you are still human. Do not neglect yourself or your family.

- Enjoy hobbies and other interests without compromising time necessary to prepare your lectures and ward rounds.

CHAPTER 13

Problems and Temptations

Like other mere human beings, the physician faces distractions and temptations along his path, and understanding them in advance is the best way to avoid falling prey to them. I served on a medical licensure board for nine years and observed young and old physicians who had made mistakes that wrecked their professional lives and that sometimes destroyed their families. One of them was a young doctor who was enticed to make a quick dollar by writing prescriptions for narcotics. His practice was thriving and he was doing well financially. But he wanted more.

His adventure in greed ended when he wrote a prescription for a narcotics agent. His license was revoked for the mandatory eight years and he served prison time for four years. When he applied to regain his license, the board required that he pass a licensure exam. He had been out of training for ten or more years, and failed the exam, even after several attempts. He never practiced again. In fact, I know of only one physician who passed the board under similar circumstances and returned to practice.

The moral of his story is perfectly obvious: Do not follow his path. And, keep in your mind that when temptation comes, it is just that: a powerful attraction to do something you know is wrong. That's why a doctor must keep his or her conscience honed to a fine edge.

And that's why I think it's crucial that medical students be required to attend two or more meetings of the licensure board. Doing so would certainly awaken them to the potential problems that await them.

Temptation isn't limited to selling drugs. Drinking alcohol while on call may be equally devastating. Dr. X, a busy obstetrician, reported for a delivery after drinking several beers. He had one too many and was inebriated. When one of the nurses reported him to the nursing supervisor, the supervisor did what she was supposed to do. She reported him to the board. Later, when Dr. X committed several similar affronts, the board suspended his license and required that he enter a treatment center. It's easy to see Dr. X's offense. It's also easy to see the standards which a doctor must live up to. Do not drink alcohol when you are on duty or might soon be called on duty. If you have been drinking, be sure to sign out to a colleague. Recognize that under the influence you aren't capable of doing the work you chose. Having the thought that you can get away with a couple of drinks on the job will almost certainly mean the end of your career. A doctor who is sentenced by the review board to even a four to six months suspension will probably have to rebuild his practice, since most of his regular patients would have moved to other doctors.

Even a moral and responsible doctor can find himself in trouble. For example, an examining physician giving a breast exam may be accused of sexual molestation. That's why it is essential that you explain the procedure of a breast examination to the patient beforehand. Tell her you will squeeze the nipple for a discharge and palpate it to detect any tumors. Most women will then understand why the procedure is so important for the sake of their health.

In my practice, I usually had a female present during breast or pelvic exams, or when the patient was partially or totally disrobed. Yet, even under these circumstances, a conscientious physician might have a patient complain to the board. In such cases, the board usually chooses a female investigator to visit the doctor's office as a patient.

You don't want to get into this kind of mess. Protect your flanks. Have a female nurse or other assistant in the room with you. And, be sensitive to a patient's request if she says she doesn't wish the employee to be present. That is the patient's prerogative. But have the assistant write a note on the chart stating that the patient requested that she not be present.

Insurance claims can also be a problem. Doctors have been known to file insurance claims for examinations and treatments they did not do. Filing such a claim to any insurance group is obviously a kind of theft. By the regulations of Medicare and Medicaid, if you file a false claim and it is detected, the government will file charges against you and your license will be suspended immediately.

Will you make mistakes? Surely you will. No one is perfect, and the board understands this. But when they see a continuing pattern of some bad practice, they will act. It's their business, after all, to protect patients from any form of mistreatment.

Malpractice is another problem. Doctors who do an improper diagnosis, or prescribe a bad treatment plan, or perform bad surgery are doing malpractice. You can avoid accusations of malpractice by taking time carefully to evaluate the patient. Do not ignore *any* symptom. If the patient complains of diarrhea, do not assume that it is an enteritis (inflammation of the intestine) and send her on her way. Check the stool and do a rectal. Diarrhea may be due to blood from a peptic ulcer or a cancer. Check out all the possibilities.

Of course, you will make a mistake and fail to catch a warning sign in your diagnosis. We all do. But don't let such a mistake be the result of careless practice. It is urgently important that you do an adequate history and physical and that you order appropriate laboratory work. And, your work must be documented by dictation or written notes.

You are also required to inform patients of any potential complications from a treatment or procedure. This should be documented on the chart and the patient should sign a form that you informed her of them. A prominent trial lawyer told me that in cases where the doctor kept good records on the standard charts, listed the possible complications, and had the patient sign the document indicating that she had been informed, he never lost a case.

Physicians should also be on guard against anyone who thinks that he or she "must have one of those doctors." The individual sees money and prestige in "them thar hills." The medical student, intern, resident, fellow, and practicing physician must be aware of the signs of a would-be lover. Protect your flanks.

In a Nutshell

- Protecting your flanks means anticipating and avoiding problems.

- Take time to evaluate each patient and document your findings.

- If you and the patient are of opposite sexes, have an employee of the same sex present during the exam.

- Inform the patient of potential complications, record what you told her on the treatment document, and have her sign the document.

CHAPTER 14

Doctors Get Sick Too

For doctors, as for everyone else, an illness looks different if it is your own. I've had a chance to experience this first hand. My thyroid tumor proved to be malignant and was removed. Then, seventeen years later, the cancer reappeared, this time in my right lung, requiring that surgeons remove a lobe of the lung. Five years after that, the cancer flared up in my left lung, also requiring surgical removal of the tumor.

While I don't want to be sick—who does?—I think that these encounters with sickness made me a better physician. I became more compassionate toward my patients and showed more understanding of their families' fears. I also became more willing to grant a patient more or stronger pain medicine. In addition, I am more willing now to grant an employee's request for a few more sick days.

A doctor, although a trained scientist, often becomes more spiritual when he falls ill and prayerfully seeks guidance from his God. This is good. Prayer can remind him that he is human just as his patients are human. I heard Dr. Ben Carson, the famous pediatric neurosurgeon at Johns Hopkins Hospital speak of his own armor of spirituality as he approached surgery for prostate cancer. X-rays had suggested that the cancer might have spread to his spine. Through prayer and grace, Dr. Carson received a different interpretation of the X-rays from a new faculty member. In fact, the cancer had *not* spread to his spine, although Dr. Carson did need surgery to remove his cancerous prostate. Today, he is doing very well, with no evidence of recurrence or spread of cancer.

I, too, had an elevated prostate specific antigen (PSA) a few years ago. After thirty-five X-ray treatments, by the grace of God, I am doing well and my PSA has returned to normal. My conviction, like Dr. Carson's, is that to bring about these favorable attitudes we simply have to believe. Once developed, this spirituality seems to permeate one's beliefs and actions.

It is by the grace of God that seriously ill patients get well. We physicians are His earthly workers. Believing in this concept sincerely directs our actions and develops an optimism that may transfer to our patients. Belief also inculcates within us an even more intense desire to seek specific diagnoses and ideal therapies for our patients. Finally, belief opens us to that extra note of compassion and understanding that is part of the best medical practice.

Spiritual faith also helps to guard a doctor against the illusion that he or she is invincible and, alone, has saved a patient's life. Obviously, such a belief can inflate the ego, and an inflated ego is a dangerous commodity in a doctor as in anyone else.

If you as a doctor become ill, seek advice and make rational decisions. I am reminded of a colleague who refused to pay any attention to a rising PSA. He later died from prostate cancer that had metastasized. Doctors beware. Such medical conditions can kill you, too. You are not invincible.

Another colleague of mine was diagnosed as having had a heart attack. Despite warnings, he went out and raked leaves. He died suddenly of a massive heart attack. Still another colleague continued to smoke, although he performed autopsies daily on patients who died of lung cancer. And, I well remember the colleague who warned his patients to wear helmets when they rode their motorcycles, but did not wear one himself. He suffered a severe head injury in an accident. Yes, we must all die of something sooner or later, but we should all play by the same rules and take care of ourselves as we urge our patients to do so. Otherwise, the Umpire above may punish by calling us out at home plate.

In a Nutshell

Doctors get sick, too. Protect yourself and your patients by:

- Wearing a mask when appropriate
- Washing your hands frequently and before and after examining a patient
- Getting appropriate checkups
- Having a family doctor
- Not treating yourself.

Part IV

SOCIAL ISSUES
AND SOLUTIONS

CHAPTER 15

Disparities in Health Care

Over the years, healthcare for Blacks has been marked by tragedy and triumph. Black infant mortality is twice that of Whites. Mortality from coronary heart disease is 40 percent higher in African Americans, while stroke mortality is nearly 80 percent higher. The incidence of diabetes is seventy percent higher among African Americans, and death rates, according to the National Institutes of Health (NIH), twenty-seven percent higher. As bad as this looks, the picture is probably still grimmer, since in many African Americans, diabetes goes undiagnosed.

Health disparities like these, and there are others I could point to, have their roots even deeper than what you might think. Yes, African Americans, especially poor ones, often don't have good access to health care, and often don't have the health information they need to stay healthy or to spot disease in its early and most treatable stage. But there is something else at work here over which African Americans at present have no control. According to a January 2005 report by the American Medical Association's Council on Scientific Affairs, "even at equivalent levels of access to care, evidence suggests that racial and ethnic minorities receive lower quality and quantity of health services compared to White Americans." The report goes on to say that "patient factors may account for the least amount of variation in health care utilization, suggesting that a greater responsibility for racial and ethnic disparities in health care may fall on the system or provider. The organization of the health care system may be the most influential factor."

What is Health Disparity?

Health disparity has been defined by the director of the National Center on Minority Health and Health Disparities as differences in the overall rate of disease incidence, prevalence, morbidity, or survival rates in the minority population as compared to the health status of the general population," accompanied by "a significant disparity in quality, outcomes, cost of use of healthcare services, or access to or satisfaction with such services as compared to the general population."

In testimony as witness to a House Subcommittee in 2001, John Ruffin, Ph.D., Director of the National Center on Minority Health and Health Disparities, testified that a variety of factors contribute to disparities, and that they interact "in unsuspecting ways to cause differences in disease progression and in health outcomes." It is the mission of his Center, in alliance with its parent organization, the National Institutes of Health, to research and identify problems that contribute to disparities in diagnosis and treatment. But the Center also has more immediate aims. Its members want to increase the number of minority people who participate in their studies. The studies explore societal, cultural, and environmental dimensions of health, with the aim of identifying the risk factors that account for the continuing gap between the health of Caucasian Americans and the health of African Americans and Hispanics.

We can only hope that out of their research, may come remediation. Our hope is strengthened by former Surgeon General Dr. David Satcher's determination to testify on the subject of health disparities and keep the issue alive. In 2001, writing in the *Yale Journal of Health Policy, Law, and Ethics*, Dr. Satcher took as his premise that "the future health of America depends substantially on our success in improving the health of racial and ethnic minorities." You can't get more real than that. Realizing the dreams of Dr. Satcher and others who are fighting this battle against social injustice may not come quickly. But the more Blacks and Latinos who understand the issue, the more likely we are to see it realized. As Dr. Satcher himself says, eliminating health disparities is not just a public health challenge; it also requires that more and more of us recognize health disparities as a civil rights issue.

Infant mortality and diabetes are the most common conditions from which African Americans are more likely to die than Caucasian Americans, but disparate death rates are also evident in other illnesses as well, including hypertension and certain cancers. For all cancers, the death rate for African Americans is thirty-five percent higher than the rate for Caucasians. And just to remind you, infant mortality among African Americans is two- and-a-half times higher than for Caucasians

Sadly, I can go on and on. From the early 1960s to the early 1990s, mortality rates for Black men rose sixty-two percent and, for Black women, sixteen percent, compared to nineteen percent for men and five percent for women of all races combined. For lung cancer, age-adjusted mortality rates are thirty-two percent higher for Blacks than for all other races combined, and the death rate is twenty-seven percent higher in Blacks. For prostate cancer, mortality is more than twice that of Whites. In breast and uterine cancers, although fewer Black women than White women get the disease, the mortality rate is higher in Blacks. Now you have some sense of the sad picture. (HealthAtoZ: Your Family Health Site—*www.healthatoz. com/healthatoz/atoz/default.html*)

A SHORT HISTORY OF BLACKS AND THE U.S. HEALTHCARE SYSTEM

Health disparities detrimental to African Americans did not evolve in isolation but were influenced by historical, economic, socio-cultural, and political events. Blacks were brought to America against their will beginning in 1619. The transatlantic slave trade, especially during the middle passage, produced a mortality rate of twenty percent or more.

This high rate resulted from unsanitary conditions that caused amebic dysentery. The slaves were also exposed to new diseases when they were first brought to this continent. The new disease environment consisted of influenza, typhoid, plague, and yellow fever, all of which took their toll.

There were no laws that encouraged slave owners to provide satisfactory healthcare, although some owners did so for economic reasons and some out of compassion. But many others neglected the healthcare of their slaves. Indeed, as slavery became institutionalized, a slave health subsystem evolved, and it obviously worked poorly.

A scientifically based health system in the U.S. began when the first medical college was established as the College of Pennsylvania (later University of Pennsylvania) in 1765. Of course, there were no Blacks enrolled. The first African American to obtain a medical degree was Dr. James McCune Smith of New York, who graduated from the University of Glasgow, Scotland, in 1837. The first Black to graduate from an American medical school was David J. Peck, who earned his M.D. from Rush Medical College in Chicago in 1847. Until Howard University was established in 1868 and Meharry Medical College in 1876, Black doctors remained few and far between.

Because most schools did not accept Blacks, several additional Black medical schools, such as Louisville National Medical School and Knoxville Medical College, were established. However, after a nationwide evaluation of medical schools in the early 1900's, only the original Black schools, Howard University and Meharry College, survived.

Black physicians were not accepted into the American Medical Association (AMA) for many years. They, therefore, formed their own organization, the National Medical Association (NMA) in 1895 at the First Congregational Church in Atlanta, Georgia. Since physicians were required to be members of the AMA in order to have hospital privileges, Black doctors could not admit their patients to hospitals, and thus they were obliged to develop their own hospitals just as they had formed their own medical schools and medical organization. One of the earliest Black hospitals was Freedman's Hospital, established in Washington, D.C., for the treatment of slaves and freed slaves.

In 1891, Dr. Daniel Hale Williams in Chicago founded Provident Hospital and Training School for Nurses, as the first Negro-owned and operated hospital in America, Provident provided for the training of nurses and interns in Chicago. Negro patients were denied admission to White hospitals. Provident provided a hospital where Negro physicians could treat Negro patients.

Also in 1891, Lincoln Hospital was founded in Durham, North Carolina, by Dr. Aaron McDuffie Moore, when he convinced Washington Duke, an American tobacco industrialist and philanthropist that a hospital would be a more valuable investment than Duke's idea of building a monument on the Trinity campus to honor Negroes who had fought for the confederacy.

By 1906, there were fifty Negro hospitals and seventy-five by 1920, but the economically fragile facilities were risky and were eventually forced to close. Negro patients were admitted to the basement of certain White hospitals, and to segregated wings of other hospitals or to city hospitals, where medical students, interns, and residents cared for them as part of their training.

Such discriminatory patterns have left a legacy of disparities in medicine that persists today. These patterns also left a shortage of minority physicians. Of the 375,000 physicians in the United States in 1977, only 1.7 percent were African American. Moreover, eighty-three percent of the African American physicians were trained at two predominantly African American medical schools, Howard and Meharry. Today things have improved to the point that six percent of applicants to medical schools are African American and 6.2 percent, Hispanic. Acceptance rates today are also much improved, with 39.8 percent of African American and forty-seven percent of Hispanic applicants accepted.

OTHER CAUSES OF DISPARITY

While racism has been a key reason for health disparities, the disparities have more than one cause. Poverty is a key one. In 1996, the median income for African-American households was $23,482, $12,000 less than the average median income. Today, in American cities, child poverty rates among Black children range from thirty-five to fifty percent.

According to the latest figures issued by the Bureau of Census, poverty is on the rise again, after reaching an all-time low in 1999. (National Economic Counsel, September 26, 2000, (*www.WH/ EOP/nec/html/working_families.html*). Between 2000 and 2001, rates rose from 11.3 percent to 11.7 percent. In the same year, median household income declined 2.2 percent from its 2000 level to $42,228 in 2001 (*www.census.gov/Press-Release/www/2002/cb02-124.html*).

Many observers, including Harold Freeman, former president of the American Cancer Society, have noted that poor Blacks are too busy facing the day-to-day survival necessities, such as food and shelter, to think much about health issues. Barbara D. Powe, RN, sums the problem up this way: "Poverty", she says, breeds fatalism, and fatalism is "the categorical surrender of the human spirit to external forces of life that destroy the human personality, potential, and life." (Powe, B.D., "Cancer Fatalism Among African Americans: A Review of Literature," *Nursing Outlook*. 1996 Jan–Feb; 44(1):18-21).

Some experts see the history of Black health as the history of the brutal impact of the institution of slavery on African Americans. In *An American Health Dilemma, A Medical History of African Americans and the Problem of Race, Beginnings to 1900* (New York, N.Y.: 2000), W. Michael Byrd, MPH '92, and Linda A. Clayton, MPH '92, both gynecologists and adjunct professors of public health practice at Harvard University, catalogue the grim legacy that has left many African Americans with low expectations of their power to control their own destinies, even in matters of health. This may account for why so relatively few African Americans take their health in their own hands. By not doing so, we fail to profit from what today is known about diet and exercise, both of which have been clearly related to health and sickness.

That unfortunate legacy was hammered down, the authors argue, by a collusion of White doctors and the legal system, which generated and wove into law pseudoscientific racial inferiority theories that were used originally to justify slavery.

For a long time, thanks to these "theories," Clayton and Byrd believe that White physicians developed an ethical blind spot. Faced with the high rate of death, disease, and disability among slaves, they held that slaves did not deserve better health care than did farm animals. (In his *Narrative,* Frederick Douglass describes slaves eating from troughs similar to hog troughs.)

Even after legal slavery ended in America, there continued the idea that poor Black health was just one more example of the difference between the races—in short, it was "natural." This belief was incorporated into a system of separate and unequal medical care that remained entrenched for more than 300 years—and continues to resonate in current health practices.

POOR ACCESS

Many people simply have no way to get health care. Because there are more White Americans, the largest number of the underserved is White; however, by percentage the higher proportion is made up of minorities. To make matters worse, there is a shortage of minority physicians. Too often, language barriers and cultural insensitivity between a White doctor and a minority patient lead to stereotyping by the provider and lack of compliance by the patient.

In such cases, I call it poor access if you are unable to get care from physicians who can understand what you tell them, and who can give you instructions that *you* can understand. In addition, we all need care from practitioners who treat us with sensitivity and respect. This isn't to say that White doctors can't bring these qualities to their treatment of Black or Hispanic patients, or that minority physicians always do. But people with shared backgrounds are more likely to understand one another better and therefore may communicate more easily.

RACISM

Racism, whether perceived or actual, direct or subtle, has an enormous effect on disparities in health care. A report from the Institute of Medicine (2003) states that:

"Concern is growing. . . . that even at equivalent levels of access to care, racial and ethnic minorities experience a lower quality of health services and are less likely to receive even routine medical procedures than White Americans. For example, African Americans and Hispanics [are less likely than Whites] to receive appropriate cardiac medication. . . . or to undergo coronary artery bypass surgery, even when variations in such factors as insurance status, income, age, co-morbid conditions, and symptom expression are taken into account. African Americans with end stage renal disease are less likely to receive hemodialysis and kidney transplantation..., and African-American and Hispanic patients with bone fractures seen in hospital emergency departments are less likely than Whites to receive pain medications.

THE FUTURE

Now that disparities in healthcare have so clearly been recognized, efforts are being made to correct the situation. In the early 1990s, the board of the AMA established a commission on minority health to study the problem and make recommendations. The AMA also gave a seat in its House of Delegates to the NMA, the medical association of African-American doctors. The AMA's strategic plan is to decrease health disparities by, for example, collaborating with other African-American organizations and community groups, particularly the African-American church, for health education, health fairs, medical screenings, and affordable group insurance.

The NMA, like the AMA, stresses the importance to doctors of cultural competence. Cultural competency means, "providing patient care in consideration of ethnic characteristics that may impact types and amount of medications. It means debunking myths and misconceptions that continue to hinder proper diagnosis and treatment of disease." We're all familiar with those myths, and we can't imagine that they will go down without fighting. That's why the AMA's effort is important to us: they are doing what they can to fight for our lives, though we shouldn't expect quick changes.

The AMA, together with the Institute of Medicine, advocates programs for improving medical education of ordinary people. They also seek increased funding for the United States Department of Health and Human Services' Office of Civil Rights, a department created to enforce laws prohibiting discrimination in the health care system and to provide special funding for agencies like the National Institutes of Health (NIH). In this way the NIH has established a division to investigate disparities in healthcare.

Congress determined that there is a need for more minority physicians, scientists and researchers and has funded programs to help correct this problem. Grants have also been made available to health professionals for education and for conferences to promote culturally competent health care. At IUSM, Dr. Patricia Keener developed a program and video that enables students of diverse backgrounds to discuss health and social issues and mores with African-American community leaders, with the aim of diminishing stereotyping and poor communication. A recent freshman class orientation at IUSM had sessions in which actors portrayed patients of diverse ethnic backgrounds. These sessions were very successful in developing an atmosphere of understanding.

With the increased awareness of disparities in healthcare and with the programs that have been instituted, there is hope that the problem will be eliminated. Fundamentally, it is a question of simple justice.

In a Nutshell

- Disparities in healthcare are defined as differences in incidence, morbidity, and mortality in specific diseases between minority and White ethnic groups.

- Causes of disparities include poverty, poor access, and racism.

- To eliminate disparities, we need more minority physicians, adequate health insurance for all, and the elimination of racism.

- The National Medical Association, the American Medical Association, and the National Institute of Health have launched programs that encourage community discussions and health fairs that teach people to take more responsibility for their health.

- The most effective means of decreasing disparities is to decrease poverty.

CHAPTER 16

Affirmative Action

Minority physicians remain in short supply, and the shortage can best be corrected by affirmative action in medical school admission. While White physicians often treat minority patients with skill and sensitivity, many Black patients are more comfortable being treated by Black physicians. The cultural divide that often separates them from the White physician can result in poor communication and lack of trust between doctor and patient, and poor compliance by the patient. (Ironically, poor and uninsured patients, both Black and White, *are* commonly seen and treated by minority physicians or by medical students, interns, and residents who are studying to become practicing doctors.)

When minority patients are treated by physicians of the same race, studies show disparities are virtually eliminated. Again, cultural understanding, trust, and compliance account for this positive result. For the poor or uninsured patient, another advantage is that, while most minority physicians will accept Medicaid patients, many majority physicians will not.

As the late Reverend Dr. Martin Luther King, Jr. observed, "Of all forms of inequality, injustice in health is the most shocking and inhumane." That injustice reveals itself in a number of ways. While African Americans are fifty percent more likely to have heart attacks, they are fifty percent less likely to have coronary angioplasty and thirty-three percent less likely to have coronary artery bypass surgery. In many cases, this means they aren't getting proper treatment. We see the same pattern in kidney disease. African Americans account for thirty-three percent of all cases of kidney disease but they make up only twenty-one percent of the patients who receive kidney transplants.

Certainly, part of the problem is economic. According to the American Medical Association, twenty-five percent of African Americans have no medical insurance and twenty percent have no consistent source of health care. For them, this usually means that the *only* source of health care is the emergency room, which is usually overcrowded and rushed. As a result, many Black patients do not receive adequate care and do not receive follow-up examination and further treatment as needed.

The situation is even worse for African-American children. In 1996, 13.9 percent of Caucasian children had no health coverage. For African-American children the figure is 18.8 percent, and for Hispanic children, a soaring fact: Hispanic children are the least likely to have health insurance coverage. The situation has worsened since these figures were gathered. In the period from 1987 to 1996, the number of American children without health coverage rose from 8.2 million to 10.6 million. No nation can take pride in these figures, and, indeed, there are so-called Third World nations that care for their children better than this. *(www.census.gov/prod/3/98pubs/cenbr981.pdf)*.

Racism is certainly one reason for health disparity. *The Journal of the American Medical Association (JAMA,* May 2, 1990) reported that even when African Americans gain access to the health care system, they are less likely than Caucasian Americans to "receive certain surgical and other therapies." In other words, they get worse medical treatment than Whites.

While it certainly won't solve all health disparity problems, one specific way to attack them is to train more African-American physicians and other healthcare professionals. Often African Americans view a career in medicine as out of their reach. "Oh, I just don't have the grades," or, "I don't have the science preparation." But these days there are effective programs for helping such capable and bright young people to achieve their dream.

One does not have to be a genius to be a physician. Yes, training and practice require intelligence, but they also require equal doses of persistence and a deep desire to be compassionate and helpful. The requirement to have a high GPA and MCAT may be desirable, but it is used largely simply because there are more applicants than places in medical schools, and test scores allow easy filtering. The fact is that for many students, if they have the right stuff, the required grade scores could be lowered and still be on a level commensurate to successful medical practice.

A student with a solid "B" average, especially in the sciences, and an average MCAT can be a very good physician, especially if he or she has attributes like determination, leadership, and compassion. For example, Mary Murray attended a predominantly Black college and had a 3.5 GPA, but she scored a 15 on the MCAT (the common acceptance score is 22). Nonetheless, she was accepted into a predominantly White state medical school that had an agreement to accept the top students in Mary's college. But the committee at the medical school had other good reasons to accept Mary. She had strong leadership skills and enjoyed the respect of her peers, as reflected in the fact that she had been president of her sorority. Today, Mary is a resident in internal medicine. This is Affirmative Action working to the advantage of all. You will hear many more stories of triumph over obstacles in the chapters that follow.

A recent decision by the Supreme Court allows admission committees of medical schools to take race into consideration. This is Affirmative Action of a very pragmatic kind, because the need is so great. Affirmative Action is not aimed at forcing medical schools, or any other schools, to accept unqualified students. Under-represented minority students must have the necessary credentials. At the same time, even if you don't have the necessary qualifications upon graduation from college, it is always possible to enter postgraduate programs to strengthen your qualifications.

African-American physicians have made a proud record for themselves. The National Medical Association reports that they are more ready to practice in predominantly underserved areas and treat the poor. They also give generously of their time for free care and for worthwhile community activities. In short, they represent the very best of the profession: high competence and genuine compassion and concern. They are soldiers in the battle to provide more Americans with the high quality of health care they deserve.

PROGRAMS TO HELP YOU GET OFF TO AN EARLY START

Besides these new actions to facilitate the training of under-represented minority students in medicine, several types of programs are available to give you a head start toward becoming a doctor. The first type, for the high school student, is offered by organizations like the Center For Leadership Development (CLD) in Indianapolis, founded with the help of the Lilly Foundation. Later on in this chapter, CLD staff and alumni will describe CLD's programs in detail.

The second type is a program for college students, which allows them to work with medical students, university professors, and researchers. It has proven to be very effective in preparing college students for entry into medical school. While in such a program, Anthony Harris developed an instrument that performs a procedure in pulmonary medicine and is seeking a patent for this device. He is now a M.D. I could point to many other examples of the success of this program.

THE CENTER FOR LEADERSHIP DEVELOPMENT HIGH SCHOOL PROGRAM

Dennis Bland, CEO of CLD

States all over the country have programs aimed at high school students who want to be doctors. I'll talk here about the one I know best. In September of 2001, CLD President Dennis Bland and Michael Cross, Vice President of Administration and Curriculum, were called upon by Cynthia Holmes Gardener, board member of the Health Foundation of Greater Indianapolis, to help develop a program for increasing the number of African-American youth qualified to become medical doctors. The vision for what came to be known as the "Pre-Rawls Scholars Medicine Initiative" was developed and implemented by William E. Durham, Jr., Program Manager at CLD.

The program was named for Dr. George H. Rawls, in recognition of a career that embodies the goals of academic achievement, professional excellence, and community service. Dr. Rawls has helped generations of young African Americans into and through medical school. He has been a distinguished role model for youth in this program.

The Pre-Rawls Scholars Medicine Initiative program focuses on helping students become physicians or to enter the many other exciting career opportunities in the field of medicine. To accomplish this, the program provides education and motivation to students considering careers in medicine. Further, the program provides parents with the information and education they need in order effectively to support and guide their child from high school through medical school.

Here are the specific goals that the program sets out to achieve:

1. Identify a select group of minority youth who have expressed an interest in careers in medicine and other health professions and recruit them into the Pre-Rawls Scholars Program.

2. Provide Pre-Rawls Scholars with the knowledge and understanding of the rigorous academic requirements for admission to and success in medical school.

3. Provide participants with motivation, inspiration, education, and support from those inside and outside the medical community.

4. Develop in participants a heightened sense of confidence and belief that they have the aptitude, ability, and financial resources required to become physicians.

5. Develop a true understanding of the work ethic, sacrifice, and commitment required for admission into medical school and for effective performance there, so that they may graduate and become successful physicians.

6. Coordinate the submission of an essay (five-page minimum) written by each Pre-Rawls Scholar that describes the following:

A. What they learned from the Pre-Rawls Scholars Medicine Initiative

B. The specific knowledge, understanding, and commitment they have acquired about what it takes to become physicians

C. What and how will they give back to the minority community after they become doctors.

How the Program Works

The first session for students enrolled in the program is an orientation at which they meet and greet Dr. Rawls and listen to him as he shares his experiences and his expertise. In the sessions that follow, the scholars listen to medical students and doctors talk about the key high school courses that will lead them towards a career in medicine. There are also sessions on college pre-med courses, MCAT requirements, medical school admission, the life of a medical student, and a personalized account of the speaker's "journey to medicine."

In the following session, students tour the Indiana University School of Medicine and St. Vincent Hospital. Each tour is designed to provide the students with firsthand experience of what it's like to be a medical student and what it's like to be a doctor. For example, when touring the medical school, students sit in the lecture hall as medical students describe a typical day. Additionally, students see "live" operations in progress and have an opportunity to ask pertinent questions of the medical students and doctors.

The Center for Leadership Development believes that by exposing these youths to this "inside experience", they will gain a clearer grasp both of academic requirements and of the medical admissions process. The desired outcome is that young students come away believing, "I can and will become a doctor." This program is now funded and administered by CLD and the Wishard Foundation of Indianapolis.

The Success of the Program

Over the past years, the program has enjoyed tremendous success. In 2002, twenty-four students (eighteen women and six men), and ten parents participated in the program. The curriculum involved six three-hour sessions with a faculty of four doctors and five medical students. Each student and parent participant received eighteen hours of curriculum instruction. Through a partnership between the Indiana University Cancer Research Center and the CLD, pre-Rawls Scholar Merle Davidson was selected as a summer intern at the Indiana University Cancer Research Center.

During 2003, the program expanded the number of participants. Twenty-nine students (twenty-six women and three men) and twelve parents went through the program, and three doctors, four medical students, and one registered nurse composed the faculty. The highlight of the year was the selection of Amber Kirk, India Johnson, and Robert Branch as summer interns in the Indiana University Cancer Research Center.

Talk to your high school counselor about getting into a similar program near you.

A Program Graduate Tells His Story

Robert L. Branch, II

When I was seventeen, I entered the Center for Leadership Development (CLD) Self-Discovery Career Exploration Program, and since then I have also participated in other programs offered by CLD, including the Pre-Rawls Scholars Medicine Initiative. In CLD, I had open discussions with medical students and doctors during which I asked questions and got answers over a broad range of topics. These sessions showed me that I needed to plan if I wished to enter into a medical career. Such a plan, I discovered, was elaborate. I had to list not only the recommended classes for each year, but also include a scheme for organizing and analyzing classes into a manageable time schedule. The program also helped me to sort out myths from facts, and encouraged me to set realistic goals.

During the sessions, medical students, doctors, and other presenters were like career advisors. They opened my eyes to the sacrifices one must make in order to pursue a career in medicine. While each medical student shared his or her unique experiences during training, I was particularly impressed by Ms. Pamela Cates, a scholarship recipient for 2002, who had taken an untraditional route to medical school by majoring in English and drama as an undergraduate.

As the sessions continued, I toured the I.U. School of Medicine and learned from admissions counselors about admission requirements, along with scholarships, residencies, and fellowships that could help me finance my medical education. A session with medical students informed me what "rigorous" meant when they explained that in medical school I would need to study a minimum of five to six hours a day!

I came away from the program knowing that by applying self-discipline, maintaining a good work ethic, and cultivating strength of character I could make the road to medical school less difficult. I am thankful for what I have learned at these CLD sessions. I believe I am ready to face the challenge of reaching my aim and fulfilling my destiny of becoming a medical doctor.

CHAPTER 17

Pre-matriculation Programs

A medical school pre-matriculation program lasts between two and six weeks. It helps the student make the social, academic, and environmental adjustment to medical school, which can be an especially daunting task for disadvantaged students, including rural, minority, and non-traditional students.

Here are specific ways the program helps incoming students:

1. Assistance in acquiring housing and getting settled

2. Tour of the campus to familiarize them to their new environment

3. Meetings with their peers, faculty, administration and some upperclassmen

4. Classes to help students:

   • Manage time effectively

   • Develop learning skills

   • Learn to study in small groups after individual study

   • Learn the technique of problem-based learning

   • Take adequate notes

- Gain exposure to medical terminology and derivatives

- Listen to lectures in the basic sciences

- Learn to avoid and manage stress

- Develop good test-taking skills.

For some students, losing summer work, or even summer vacation, was a disincentive. But for most candidates, the medical students themselves proved to be the salesmen for the program, through telephone calls to recalcitrant students, emphasizing to them how the program had been shown to help reduce both failure and stress.

INDIANA UNIVERSITY'S MSMS PROGRAM
William Agbor-Baiyee, Ph.D., M.P.A.

Assistant Professor of Family Medicine and
Director, Master of Science in Medical Science Program
Director, Special Programs, Medical Student Affairs
Indiana University School of Medicine

What if you aren't accepted for admissions the first time you apply to medical school? Does that mean the end of the road? It doesn't have to, as Dr. Agbor-Baiyee's essay makes clear.

Introduction

Thousands of able and determined students apply to medical schools and not all of them are admitted. Admission is a highly competitive process. If you are one of those who do not get admitted the first time you apply, don't think your chances are over. Instead, develop a strategy to strengthen your credentials and your interviewing skills. Updated credentials demonstrate your sustained commitment to medicine as a career. Updating may mean retaking the Medical College Admission Test (MCAT), or it may mean improving your grade point average (GPA) by taking further courses in the biomedical sciences or repeating courses you have already taken. It may even mean that you must meet both challenges before you reach your goal of admission.

A number of U.S. colleges and universities have programs designed to assist students to improve their academic credentials for admission to medical school. Some schools offer postgraduate programs that include classes in the premedical sciences, MCAT preparation, and premedical advisement. Some premedical graduate programs offer a certificate while others offer a master's degree. Some of these programs are designed to help medical schools attract disadvantaged students as a means to diversify their student bodies.

This chapter discusses the Master of Science in Medical Science (MSMS) Program at Indiana University School of Medicine as a model academic pathway for unsuccessful medical school applicants.

Master of Science in Medical Science Program

A faculty committee in 1994 reviewed the recruitment and retention of disadvantaged and under-represented minority students at Indiana University School of Medicine (IUSM). The committee recommended the formation of a premedical graduate degree-granting program. The committee's recommendation took into account the experience of medical schools such as Wayne State University School of Medicine, Southern Illinois University School of Medicine, and Michigan State University, each of which offer successful premedical postgraduate programs. The Master of Science in Medical Science (MSMS) Program at IUSM was established in 1995.

The two-year MSMS Program was established to provide students from disadvantaged backgrounds with the opportunity to develop into confident and prepared people ready for the challenges of medical school and the practice of medicine. The program includes thirty-five credit hours of coursework at the graduate level in courses that provide experiences in didactic instruction, problem-based learning, and research. All admitted students are required to complete an intensive summer Medical College Admission Test Preparation Program offered at IU School of Medicine before starting. Students who maintain a GPA of 3.0 graduate with a Master of Science in Medical Science degree.

Three goals drive the program. First, it seeks to increase the diversity of Indiana University School of Medicine's student body. Second, through its graduate level instructional program in the basic medical sciences, the program seeks to promote the future academic success of our students once they enter medical school itself. Finally, the program helps get the disadvantaged student into and through medical school. Students in the program are advised not to take on part-time work. They will need all the time they can get keeping up with their coursework.

Who is Eligible?

The MSMS admissions process looks closely at both a student's academic potential and financial and educational background. Applicants must be U.S. citizens or permanent residents. Family income levels, as defined by the federal government, are used to evaluate economic disadvantage. Before they may enter the MSMS Program, applicants must have a bachelor's degree from an accredited institution in the U.S. or an equivalent international institution, with a minimum cumulative and science GPA of 3.0, and they must have completed all premedical science requirements (one year of general biology, chemistry, organic chemistry, and physics, with laboratory components). In addition, applicants must have achieved at least a five on the physical sciences, verbal reasoning, and biological sciences sections of the MCAT).

Selection

The admissions committee at IUSM has responsibility to select MSMS students from its pool of applicants to participate in the program. Each application for admission cycle starts on October 15 and ends on March 15. In order to avoid delays in reviewing applications, candidates are advised to submit application materials to the program as early as possible.

Based upon the evaluation of the application, an applicant may be invited for a personal interview. Interviewers will probe and evaluate the student's:

- Motivation for a medical career

- Suitability for the MSMS Program

- Attitude toward entering a graduate program designed to strengthen each student's required competencies

- Academic record, including performance in undergraduate and, if appropriate, postgraduate work

- Community involvement and exposure to medicine.

Applicants who are invited to interview are responsible for travel and lodging costs.

Following the interview, the MSMS admissions advisory committee reviews the application. The committee then, after discussing each case, recommends successful candidates to the executive and review committee, which serves as the MSMS admissions committee.

Elements of the Program

The components of the program include an intensive, summer, ten-week undergraduate experience to prepare for the Medical College Admission Test (MCAT) and a graduate academic experience in medical science that includes twenty-eight credit hours of didactic instruction, four credit hours of problem based learning, and three credit hours of guided research.

MCAT Preparation Program

MCAT scores are critical for admission to medical school. Although this required 10-week summer academic experience is not a part of the graduate curriculum, it is a key foundational experience for MSMS students. The program includes physical sciences, biological sciences, critical reading and writing, and problem-based learning sessions. Total immersion in a concentrated learning environment, focused on improving MCAT performance, permits students to develop skills and habits that carry over into other academic endeavors and serve them well for life.

The MCAT Preparation Program takes a holistic view of student learning. Students, tutors, and instructors are an integrated team that strives to facilitate the personal growth upon which students can build the positive attitudes that make possible a strong command of content and new test-taking skills. The program's core belief is that a positive and confidence-building context enhances the student's sense of ownership of the learning process. We try to establish a learning atmosphere in which cooperation, respect, integrity, excellence, creativity, and autonomy flourish.

The curriculum for MCAT preparation includes biology (six hours per week), general chemistry (six hours per week), organic chemistry (six hours per week), physics (six hours per week), verbal reasoning (six hours per week), and writing (1.5 hours per week). Students are involved in structured instruction five days per week. Instruction by experienced teachers, who also have completed the first year of medical school, consists of formal lectures and practice MCAT passage-solving. Students also meet in small groups for three hours three times per week to solve practice MCAT passages, applying problem-based learning principles.

After each class session of biology, general chemistry, organic chemistry, physics, and verbal reasoning, students are assigned an appropriate MCAT passage. Students work not only to find a solution to the passage but also to explain in writing the reasoning process that led them to that solution. Answers are discussed during the next class session. Five full-length practice MCATs (4 hours and 20 minutes of content time per test) are administered on Saturdays during the ten-week preparation period. The practice tests enable students to measure their progress, practice test-taking strategies, and master the format of the MCAT.

Graduate Biomedical Science Program

A two-year rigorous academic program is employed to prepare MSMS students for the medical curriculum. The thirty-five credit hours graduate academic experience in medical science includes twenty-eight credit hours of didactic instruction, four credit hours of problem based learning, and three credit hours of guided research.

Students who excel in the first year of the program are typically admitted to medical school. Some students who go on to complete the second year and obtain the degree, are admitted to medical school.

The first-year curriculum includes basic histology, introduction to biochemistry, physiology, human gross anatomy, microbiology, and problem-based learning in medical science. These courses build a fund of knowledge in basic science that can be applied to clinical situations in the problem-based learning course. Extensive laboratory-based learning is done in basic histology and human gross anatomy to deepen the student's understanding of human form and function, from the molecular to the whole body level. The quantity and quality of the didactic courses mimic those common of the first year medical school curriculum and enhance the student's study skills and ability to digest volumes of information.

The second year curriculum includes regenerative biological and medicine, neuroanatomy, pharmacology, genetics, and guided research in medical science. The didactic courses further expand the student's knowledge of basic science used in clinical practice. The guided research experience develops the student's critical thinking skills and enhances written and oral communication skills. The guided research is an independent basic science research project conducted under the direction of a faculty mentor; it enhances students' intellectual and technical skills in an area of their interest.

As you can see, once a student enters the program, he is supported in every way possible. So far, Indiana University School of Medicine has awarded sixty two (34%)) MSMS degrees. This is relatively low given that 50% of students leave for medical school after the first year in the program.

Program Outcomes

The MSMS Program has been successful in helping students gain admission and graduate from the medical program at IU School of Medicine. Participants of the program improve their performance not only on the MCAT but also in the graduate biomedical science curriculum. Students from the program who matriculated in medical school have been better prepared for the challenges of the medical curriculum.

Since its inception in 1995, 230 students of an average age of twenty-four have participated in the program. While one hundred two (44%) of the participants have been residents of Indiana, one hundred twenty eight (56%) have come from other states. In terms of gender one hundred fifty two (66%) of participants have been female while seventy eight (34%) have been male. Participants have come from diverse backgrounds including one hundred ninety one (83%) African American, two (1%) Native American, nineteen (8%) Hispanic, thirteen (6%) Caucasian, and five (2%) Asian/Pacific Islander.

From 1995 to 2006, one hundred forty nine (71%) of our students have been admitted to IU School of Medicine and other medical schools. Of the one hundred forty eight admitted to medical schools eighty two (39%) matriculated at IU School of Medicine, while sixty seven (32%) went to other medical schools; one hundred six (50%) of those who gained admission were admitted following the first year in the program, while forty three (21%) were admitted following two years in the program.

We shift our focus to our students admitted in the medical program at IU School of Medicine for whom the program was originally designed. In addition, privacy concerns limit the willingness of academic records offices to share data on the academic performance and progress of our students attending other medical schools.

Of the eighty two MSMS participants who gained admission to IU School of Medicine from 1995 to 2006 forty eight (59%) were Indiana residents compared to thirty four (41%) from other states. The gender distribution was fifty four (66%) were female and twenty eight (34%) were male. While sixty three (77%) were offered IU School of Medicine admission after one year in the program, nineteen (23%) were offered medical school after two years in the program.

In terms of ethnicity, sixty four (78%) African American students, seven (9%) Hispanic students, one (1%) Native American student, eight (10%) Caucasian students, and two (2%) Asian/Pacific Islander students from the MSMS Program were admitted in the medical program at Indiana University School of Medicine.

We know that only five percent of former MSMS participants have dropped out of the medical program at IU School of Medicine.

They were dismissed on grounds of poor academic performance or withdrew for personal reasons. Thirty eight IU School of Medicine MD degrees have been awarded to formed MSMS students.

Program Administration

The program is administered at three main levels:

1. A Director aided by staff, manages the daily operations of the program

2. The Executive Associate Dean for Educational Affairs ensures that the program complies with the academic standards of IU School of Medicine, and

3. The Faculty Advisory Committee ensures that the program curriculum is relevant and challenging and provides oversight of the program's academic policy and of student progress.

Psychological Support

The academic program also fosters the psychosocial development of its students. Besides a one-day orientation and a one-week Student Success Seminar for new students, it also provides advice throughout the academic year. The program director and the faculty counsel students who encounter difficulties and refer them to appropriate campus resources for further assistance. Regular program meetings are organized to discuss developmental issues. Students are involved in program evaluation, peer tutorials, and focused faculty-student interactions.

Summing Up

The MSMS program has met its purpose of expanding the pool of successful medical school applicants from disadvantaged backgrounds. The program addresses the need of most of its students for higher performance on the MCAT through the required ten-week intensive summer undergraduate program to prepare for the test. The MCAT preparation provides MSMS participants with foundational academic experience that emphasizes test taking, time management, and study skills. Students with low undergraduate GPAs have the opportunity to enhance their academic credentials through the rigorous graduate biomedical science curriculum. Thus, the graduate MSMS curriculum builds on the MCAT preparation, providing a thorough preparation for success in a medical curriculum.

The MSMS program has increased the number of successful applicants from especially disadvantaged backgrounds. These students are more likely to return to serve as physicians in underserved communities with corresponding benefits to public health.

Although the MSMS Program's primary emphasis is on preparing participants for success in a medical curriculum, students who are not successful in gaining medical school admission are provided appropriate career advisement. Such counseling has resulted in these students being placed in other graduate professional programs, such as law, public health, education, and physicians' assistant programs.

Our program allows students to learn, and practice more effective skills for higher academic performance—skills necessary for admission to, and success in a medical program. Students who are admitted to medical schools have demonstrated their readiness to succeed through discipline, focus, study, and time management that they may have lacked when they matriculated in the program.

Although former MSMS students come to IU School of Medicine with lower undergraduate grade-point averages and MCAT scores than do students outside the program, sixty-eight percent of its graduates are enrolled in medical schools. Retention of program graduates at IU School of Medicine is excellent (96 percent), especially when we consider that these students had difficulty gaining admission to medical school prior to matriculating in the MSMS Program. As the program grows, it will continue to evaluate its design and operational strategies. It will continue to employ student and faculty evaluation data to make appropriate improvements. Challenges that it faces include recruiting more residents of Indiana, enhancing efforts to cultivate a positive and strong programmatic identity both in and out of state, and obtaining funds for scholarships to supplement student loans.

Chapter 18

Women in Medicine

Bettye-Jo Rawls Lloyd, M.D.

In the Beginning

I was always ambitious. In elementary school, I had my life planned: I would become a teacher. What the heck, I liked kids and I admired several of my teachers. By fifth grade, my first career choice was challenged. Our assignment was to write an essay on "What do you want to become when you grow up and why? (Thanks, Mrs. Moss.) Now, that took some genuine soul searching for a ten year-old.

What I came up with is that I wanted to choose an occupation that was altruistic, rewarding, and meaningful, and I needed to have a terrific reason for my choice. Then it became obvious. Why, I'd go into medicine. You see, my father (my hero) was a physician. In those days, medicine was a male-dominated field, but my father had no sons, and there I was, to help carry on his footsteps.

What a topic, what a paper, what a grade!! My teacher was ecstatic and shared this news with everyone. I was a "good student" and I worked hard. That was my first academic triumph, and it encouraged me throughout elementary school to expect success and get it. Of course, I had no real understanding of the challenges I would face. What I did understand was that preparation plus opportunity equaled success, and I knew that our family values included determination and perseverance in all goals. I was on my way.

A High School Student Looks Ahead

By the time I reached high school, the answer to the "What will you do when you grow up?" had become concrete. I had moved on to the question of what area of medicine in which to specialize. After discussing it with several doctors and doing additional research on my own, I decided I would go into radiology. This field seemed to combine the best of science and technology with diagnosis and patient care—*and,* I was told, it was a good area for a woman.

I understood that to make myself an attractive candidate for medical school required my getting into a top-notch undergraduate school. So in high school, besides keeping my grades up, I was active in school activities, and held leadership positions in student government. I also was involved in church and youth religious activities, as well as scouting. I knew that admissions committees looked for leadership qualities along with academic superiority.

As a high school junior, I had several life-altering opportunities (opportunity favors the prepared mind). The first was that for two years I was an explorer scout in medicine. I was thus exposed to medical students, interns, and residents who spoke to us regarding their experiences. In addition, I was allowed to make my first trip into an operating room and found this visit most exciting.

During my junior year, the high school parent-teacher association (spearheaded by my mom and our guidance department) initiated "Career Day." Counselors from colleges and graduate programs were brought in to meet with us. There I met Mr. Jay Michael Smith, a recruiter from Indiana University School of Medicine, who had a wealth of information about preparing for and getting into medical school. That was the beginning of a beautiful friendship. Four years later, when I was a junior in college, he would act as a major guide and resource, assisting me with choosing required classes, as well as obtaining information on how and when to take the MCAT, and on the application process to medical school.

My high school experience ended as it began—with a commitment to excellence. I took challenging courses, including all the math and science classes my schedule would allow. In most of these classes, I was the only female and, in all, the only African-American female. I was undaunted. At that stage in my life, the world was still small. My support system was encompassing and strong, and my faith and belief in myself had not been challenged. Although some people who learned that I desired to become a physician questioned whether I could or would, I had no doubts.

College Confirms My Path

I chose to matriculate at Northwestern University in Evanston, Illinois. Surrounded by some of the best and brightest students in the nation, all of whom were number one in their high schools and half of whom aspired to become physicians, I was faced with brilliant competition and was forced to learn about myself. Who was I? Why was I there? What was my passion? But I also was fascinated by the "hows" and "whys" of the universe itself, and toward that end math, science, and especially physics, were useful to me.

Again, I was faced with career choices. During that freshman year in college, professors directed me toward the research/academic path rather than towards pre-med. Was it because I am a woman or because I am Black? I may never know. My husband, who recently had an opportunity to mentor college students, told me the story of a senior Black Miami University coed with a 3.85 GPA who was counseled to apply to the physical therapy program at Indiana University rather than to medical school, as she desired.

After I'd completed a particularly grueling set of finals, I remember being told by an advisor that nursing might be an area I should explore. When I told this to my father, he said that he had had the pleasure of working with many outstanding women nurses, and that any of them would also have made equally outstanding physicians, but he knew that my own goal was to become a doctor.

Despite my advisor, I remained confirmed in my choice. That's when Jay Michael Smith reappeared, reviewed my course curriculum and identified courses I needed to take to satisfy admission requirements to medical school. I made every effort to maintain my GPA and developed a small study group of pre-med students. I tried to achieve a balance between gaining the best that college had to offer and giving the best of myself. During my undergraduate years, I also realized the power of prayer.

My boyfriend who was attending college elsewhere, told me during my senior year that he, too, was committed to pursuing medicine as a career. We decided that the relationship was serious. Pre-med couples who are considering marriage must also think about which medical schools offer programs that fit the plans of them both, along with location, cost, financial aid considerations, and which school offer both students the best opportunity to gain admittance. Both of us researched different schools, applied to, and were interviewed by several to which we were most attracted. Then we narrowed our field to schools that accepted both of us and that we could afford.

MEDICAL SCHOOL

Ironically, though we attended the same medical school, my fiancé and I were apart during our first year. Indiana University has eight campuses and we were accepted into different programs. This arrangement was probably to our advantage. The first two years of medical school are devoted to the basic sciences and require discipline and dedication to core scientific material, and although this curriculum is key to medical understanding, it does not bear directly on what a physician does. The basic science courses require the student to swallow and digest many facts, and to do so, the student must manage her time carefully. (At this time I didn't realize how much strain raising a family would put on that time management.) Courses were eight hours a day, with labs, assignments, tests, and required volumes of study. Despite my undergraduate preparation, the material was new and classes moved quickly because there was so much to cover. Most of us were committed to our decisions to become physicians and to practice medicine, but the pre-clinical years were humbling, though necessary steps that few of us could have imagined.

There were perhaps forty women in my class of more than 300. Several of the women were wives and some were mothers. We women tended to cluster together. I listened at breaks as the wives recounted their stories about preparing dinner for their husbands, doing laundry, and arranging for their children's day care. The responsibilities of family life, although simple enough for most young wives, for medical students were compounded by the amount and intensity of academic work necessary to succeed. Several wives were disgruntled because they received little support from their spouses, either emotional or otherwise. They often suffered from a feeling that their husbands didn't take in their situation. Some were overwhelmed by their responsibilities. One mother took a leave of absence because of the extended illness of one of her children. To this day, I don't know if she ever returned to finish.

Medical school in the 1970s reflected the sexist bias of the times. During classes, we were repeatedly reminded that the medical school was a public institution supported by tax dollars, and that some of us would choose to waste that money by becoming "stay at home moms" or "part-time mommy docs." I resented this remark, which I found patronizing, but, even if that *was* the mold, I made up my mind to break it.

If dedication was the theme of my first year, my second year centered around balancing dedication and relationship. My fiancé also entered the medical program, after I had completed my first year, and the year was a tightrope act. My fiancé and I learned to make sacrifices and compromises, along with decisions regarding how much time to study before we spent time together and whether we should study together. We knew that there would be no time left over for a social life.

A medical student considering getting married or entering into some other long-range arrangement, should take into account that she may not have much time left for the relationship itself. You must understand the level of drive, energy, and love needed to study and then practice medicine. If both partners are medical students, a large part of their time will go into their studies. If your partner is an attorney or businessman, you can't always give him the support he'd prefer, like accompanying him on a business trip or attending a ceremonial dinner.

As our clinical rotations approached, we felt more comfortable with our relationship, knowing that we would now have more control over our schedules. We married in our junior year. Our rotations allowed us to determine areas of interest. Although there are no longer areas that are "not for women," a female medical student's lifestyle and the skill with which she manages time and priorities will be reflected in her field of medicine. Primary care requires more hands-on patient care in the long run. Specialty residencies are more competitive and require four or more years to complete, but they may allow more flexibility, since the specialist tends to be in less constant demand than the general practitioner. Keep in mind also that choices of specialty may also mean different places of residency.

My husband and I reviewed the typical pluses and minuses of individual residency programs. I knew that attending a high profile, high-powered, and intense program, while rewarding, could also delay my decision for pregnancy and motherhood or make it more challenging. Our situation required finding programs in the same university or at least close to one another. We had decided against the commute or long-distance route.

BEING A DOCTOR

I was a surgery intern constantly on call. This was before the AMA limited a resident's hours to eighty. (Can you remember how the unions once fought for a forty-hour week?) It was my first week as an intern and I had gotten virtually no sleep for days, as I peered out of the hospital window at the top of the Washington Monument. It was 3:00 A.M. and I was at the bedside of a neurosurgical patient who was having seizures that, for the past thirty minutes, I had been trying to control. That's when I had a revelation. I realized that no one and no amount of money could make me endure this voluntarily.

Today, though the working hours have been lessened, the resident still needs all the time and energy she can muster. I was fortunate in that I trained at Howard University Hospital with some of the best and brightest—and they looked like me. These Black women were my role models. They were in every stage of relationship (and non relationship)—single, engaged, married, pregnant, or with babies and/or older children. They were my support and they encouraged me by showing that what they were doing can be done and done well. I received advice from them regarding timing of pregnancies, what kinds of rotations are best concerning call obligations and logistics, what insurance coverage I would need, how to combine and accrue sick and vacation time for leave, and other practical information that I didn't even know I needed.

Timing a marriage or pregnancy is important—that is, in situations where you have at least some degree of control. All four years of college and at least the first three years of medical school require a great deal of study and achievement of respectable grades in order for one to move to the next step. The fourth year of medical school allows at least a degree of flexibility that permits marriage or childbirth. The rigors of internship would be less ideal. The residency years afterward would also afford opportunities to commit to family.

I have heard horror stories about male physicians who bluntly or obliquely caution female residents not to get pregnant so that pregnancy would not affect the call schedule. One female internist shared with me that her attending physician had blurted, angrily, *"Are you pregnant again?"*

I became pregnant during the end of my internship. I was warned by a female attending physician not to share my news of pregnancy with the men of the department so that my transition into the first year of the residency program would be smooth. The superwoman mentality was prevalent during that era, and I was reminded that it would be best for me and for everyone else not to get caught up in that dangerous spiral of trying to do it all. My best defense from that was my spirituality, which reminded me that I hadn't been put here to control my destiny alone.

Life after residency is the dream of everyone in training, but in the midst of the new freedom there are, of course, new decisions to make. With my personality, career goals, and obligations to my family, what sort of practice should I choose? The autonomy of solo private practice is enticing (I would be able to arrange my schedule to make all of my son's field trips), but there is a problematic side: you must be able to manage a business, and working alone, it may be harder for you to keep up with the newest information. A young doctor who is leaning toward group practice must be sure that he or she can get along in a group mentality. Further, while the HMOs allow you the luxury of working only from 9a.m. to 5p.m. they sometimes impose restrictions on how you practice, whom you treat, and whom you may refer to other specialists. I chose to join a group.

Looking back, I see that my path had always led me to become an ophthalmologist. I suffered from progressive myopia and so I needed to understand vision. In addition, I had a childhood playmate who had suffered a serious sight-threatening disease. I was side-tracked in medical school by a love for pediatrics, which meant working with children and enjoying the camaraderie of personable, warm physicians. That was until I spent two months doing pediatric neonatology. As I spent all night working towards saving a two-pound infant only to lose it the next day, I realized that, while I loved working with children, it was physically and emotionally draining to work with sick ones.

As I re-explored, I revisited the option of ophthalmology, despite its being a White male-dominated field at that time (my medical school had never had a female resident complete the program), and I made the decision based on my interests. Ophthalmology is a technologically fascinating profession. It involves male and female patients of all age groups, and it gives the immediate gratification of restoring, preserving, and improving people's vision.

This specialty also would allow me some flexibility in controlling my schedule and allow me to manage a family life—or so I thought, until I began the work and heard my children's views about, say, our lost Fourth of July backyard picnic when I was called in an emergency to surgically repair an eye that had been damaged by an exploding firecracker. Worse yet were the occasions when I had been up all night nursing one or both of my children who had a temperature or uncontrollable vomiting, and then went in to work, trying to provide patient care as if everything was normal.

Yes, being a wife and being a physician has its special set of challenges. Making the balance work depends on having a spouse who understands and supports the hard work it took to get through medical school, as well as the commitment and dedication to patient care that it takes to practice medicine. Most wives agree that it would be helpful to *have* a "wife." A husband who shares in the household duties and childcare helps fill that bill. Having family and friends who are involved in the childrens' many activities also helps a lot. Additional help in the form of housekeepers, cooks, and nannies has been invaluable for me at different times in my career. As I look back, I can hardly count all the people who made my tough journey possible.

With their help, I enjoyed the best of all worlds. I played my active part in family life, and I also experienced a satisfying career—satisfying yes, but predictable, no. During my specialized training after internship, I was in charge of an ophthalmology residency clinic and supervised the training program. I oversaw the residents' surgical skills and I was responsible for their general evaluation.

Later, I moved to be near my parents, and started a private practice. After eight years, the burgeoning costs of running and managing a private practice, along with keeping up with Medicare and Medicaid rules and exercising business acumen, became too much for me and I joined a group. For three years, I was an employee and for five years, a partner in my group. Then I became an employee of a different group.

Working as part of a group has its disadvantages. When more than one person is involved, each has to engage in the politics of controlling a group venture. That can sometimes be frustrating. On the other hand, in a group, I am able to practice medicine without also having to take care of employees, payrolls, regulations, and so on. Each doctor must decide for herself which of these options proves the more comfortable.

OTHER WOMEN'S EXPERIENCES

According to the American Association of Medical Colleges, the number of women applying to medical schools over the past thirty years has risen thirty percent. Half of all Black applicants were female in 1984. By 2001, this percentage had risen to sixty-one, a figure that reflects the increasing population of Black women graduating from undergraduate programs.

As I reflected upon my own medical journey, I spoke with a range of Black female students who, like me, were very interested in knowing how women who preceded them had managed. I then interviewed a number of Black female physicians in varying stages of their careers. I came away with deep admiration for these women who followed their individual path over obstacles and pitfalls.

Many of these women knew while they were still in grade school that they would make great physicians, and most had made up their minds by late high school or early college. Several recalled teachers expressing surprise that they were choosing medicine instead of nursing, and also remembered how discouraging they found that surprise. Of the women who did not matriculate directly from college into medical school, some chose to marry and have children first; others were unsuccessful in their first attempt to enter medical school. Either way they felt disappointed when they were advised to marry and have children, or not to pursue medical school because of their families. Nevertheless, these women successfully persevered.

One of the women I talked to married early in medical school. She cited her husband as one of the sources of her success. He was the son of two physicians, and he provided her with encouragement and support. She chose well. She used her marriage as an opportunity. In her effort to spend time with her husband and at the same time, keep up with her studies, she became better at her time management and study skills.

One woman who became pregnant in the second semester of her first year in medical school faced an especially stiff challenge. Her pregnancy proved complicated, and after a glowing first semester she failed several courses. But still, she would not give up on her dream and managed to convince the academic review committee to allow her pregnancy leave as well as an opportunity to make up the failed courses during the summer. She went on to become a stellar medical school student.

A woman who decided to do her medical training *after* becoming a wife and mother spoke of the effort and will it took to re-energize herself to apply for medical school. During her first year, she felt that some of her professors and fellow students viewed her as being less dedicated than women who were single. Despite this, she did well.

She recalls being called to task by a Black female dean at the medical school (who later became her mentor). The dean reminded her that she had been the first Black female to receive a special scholarship and that she represented not only herself but also the future of every Black student who would follow. She redoubled her efforts and, despite a miscarriage in her third year, graduated with honors, published papers, and won honors from the American Osteopathic Association.

Many of us had experienced the frustrations of sexist comments from patients and attending staff. People would bluntly ask, "How can you be a physician and have kids?" Most of us were intimidated at some point by the thought that we might have to take time from our practices because of pregnancy, sick children or both. We were made to feel that some patients doubted our commitment.

ADVICE

The good news is that all of the women I interviewed would do it all over again if given the choice, and they all had similar advice:

- Start early. Don't waste those college years. Enjoy yourself but study hard. You'll have a better chance of getting into the school of your choice the first time.

- Take the chosen path seriously. Stay committed.

- Have a mentor. Many said that having a Black female physician as a mentor gave them added confidence in making decisions.

- Get support from your spouse, friends, church, or relatives. What you are doing is difficult, and some of the weight will be lifted if you have others who can urge you on and provide help, emotional or other, when you need it.

- See your role as a Black female as a positive. You may be the only female or certainly the only Black female in your lab or in groups. You will physically "stand out." Make this a positively memorable experience. Rise to the challenge.

- Be organized. Study efficiently so that you can make time for everything else.

- Manage your time and prioritize.

- Have a stress outlet, but don't let that outlet be alcohol or drugs, which could end your chance of a medical career. Effective outlets may include, for example, participation in a choir or other church-related activity, cycling or other physical activities, meditation or yoga, even shopping, if that helps you relieve tension. The key is to find an activity that lets you think about something other than medical school and that doesn't create additional stress.

- Spend some of your time with non-medical people, who will have different perspectives on life.

- Go for your goals. Certainly family members are priorities, but don't forget your passion to achieve your highest goals. Look for options and work for scholarships. You can do it! Don't let anyone tell you that you can't.

- Don't let "mommy guilt" get in your way. Being a full-time primary role model and mother, along with being a medical student or practitioner, can be a tough balancing act, but others have done it, and you can too.

- Be patient as a student and resident. Life will be more gratifying later.

- Accept that, as a Black wife and mother, you will probably need to try harder than your colleagues. Let that be a challenge to which you know you can rise.

CHAPTER 19

The Doctor's Spouse

Back in 1959, when Dr. Rawls came to Indianapolis to practice surgery, his wife and he spent a pleasant evening in the company of one of his new colleagues. At the end of the evening, the colleague's wife told him that his wife, Lula, " is smart and has a wonderful personality. She will be your most valuable asset."

Some years later, that lesson was reinforced when the Rawls' youngest daughter, then in college, remarked at the dinner table, "Mom, you're the one that makes this family tick." Dr. Rawls had thought that he "was the one who made the family tick." After all, wasn't he the doctor? How wrong he was. Without his wife at his side, at home and, often, in his office, his own work would have been impossible. For that reason, Dr. Rawls invited Lula Rawls to tell in her own words what the role of a doctor's wife feels like—to one woman, at least. If you are thinking of marrying a doctor, Lu's plain talk may help you decide if that's a role that would suit you.

LU'S STORY

The wife or husband is there to help his or her mate to make it. I always prayed to the Lord to "help George and use him in Thy service." If this happened, I knew everything would be all right. When George and I married, I was a schoolteacher and supported him with encouragement and with the few dollars I earned by teaching in

Hollywood, Florida. Later, I taught school in Dayton, Ohio, while he did his residency, and during the first year of his practice in Indianapolis. Although teachers' salaries were low, the few dollars I brought to the table did help.

Most young families will start a family as we did. The spouse must do a lot of the family's work herself, because the student, resident or young physician is busy with long hours of study and work. Sometimes it requires taking the children for a walk so the spouse can have the quiet he needs, sometimes it means going to Sunday school or church or social events alone.

The hours apart from your spouse can be long and lonely, but your responsibility if you are a stay-at-home mom is to make the most of them. When he is home, have meals ready in advance so you can play with the kids together, if only briefly. If he is studying for the boards, keep the children busy and quiet. A medical student or doctor needs your support, and sometimes you may find yourself playing a sort of cheerleader to urge him on.

In the lean times, keep the budget down so the family doesn't fall into debt. Economizing may require living in a small apartment or preparing meals with only the basic ingredients and no frills. But you can always look forward to the days when the family will live a little better, and you can always feel good about your spouse's having so worthwhile a profession: serving the sick.

When we attended our first National Medical Association (NMA) meeting in 1965, six years after George opened his office, he wanted to go on the post-convention tour but did not have the money. Luckily, I had saved some money by economizing in such ways as using coupons when shopping for food, so we had just enough to all go on our first big trip—a tour of The Netherlands. The three girls had a great time and made many friends. From then on, we regularly budgeted for the post-convention tours, which became our annual two-week vacation. Over the years, we went to Italy, Hawaii, Japan, China, Bahamas, Israel, South America, and Canada. I mention this only to suggest that even in the lean times you can find ways to give your family the recreation it needs. Trips like those we took strengthened our family bonds.

Early on, we joined Witherspoon Presbyterian Church and attended as a family. We worked in the church and attended Sunday school and vacation Bible school and participated in other church activities. These activities helped to mold us as a family. Girl Scouting and Jack and Jill organization activities were also helpful in molding our children.

Your spouse won't be able to attend all the children's extracurricular activities at school or always help with homework. But it's important that these things be done. The children will appreciate their father or mother for making such efforts.

The spouse can almost always sense tense situations—for example, surgery that did not go well or an unexpected death. She should share in the sorrow even though she does not know the patient or the details. George never discussed patients and their diseases or problems, but I always could read the "vibes." I would show my sympathy and concern by preparing a good meal or taking him out to eat or to a movie. In that way, we enjoyed a kind of solidarity over problems, even when we didn't talk about them directly.

A spouse is sometimes called to the office to fill in for a secretary or nurse who has fallen ill, so she should get to know the office routines and the patients. These roles came easily to me because I had always wanted to be a nurse, and George says that I would have been a good one because of my genuine concern. Because I got to know many of George's patients by helping in the office, I communicated with them better when I answered the phone, whether in the office or at home.

For all the arrangements a doctor's family may make to keep everything running smoothly, illness can come to doctors as it comes to anyone else. Sometimes we forget that healers can get sick just as their patients do. The touchy problem is that he knows all about the illness, its problems, and the mortality rates. I remember when George found a tumor on his neck. He could quote the percentage likelihood of its being cancer, and he knew the possible complications of the surgery for thyroid removal. I heard him talk about how injury to a nerve in surgery could cause hoarseness, and how accidental removal of some other small glands could result in other problems. We discussed these potential problems and prayed over them. I knew that his daughters would take it very hard but we had to face it. Although the experience was harrowing, it drew us all closer. It turned out that the tumor was malignant, so George had to have his entire thyroid removed. Through that experience, too, we grew closer as a family through God's guidance.

After surgery, George tired easily despite thyroid replacement medicine, and arranged to come home daily from work in the middle of the day to rest in bed. Again, my understanding and support were paramount. It was not until fifteen or more years later that researchers discovered this medicine should be taken on an empty stomach. George had always taken it at breakfast so he would not forget. Once he began taking it in the middle of the night so that it would be absorbed before eating, he felt much less tired.

Unfortunately, the tumor returned, this time to his lungs. However, his endocrinologist, Dr. Schnute, was on top of it and had surgery performed to remove a portion of his lung. Again, the girls and I were always there to give our support and offer our prayers. There were other illnesses, too. A rising PSA (prostate specific antigen) level required biopsies of the prostate twice and later specific treatment. I found that patience, understanding, and spiritual belief eases the burden of sickness.

Yes, the physician or spouse can get sick, too, sometimes with a chronic illness, like arthritis or diabetes. Partners in the good life must also be partners of misfortune and disaster, "until death do us part." Trust, honesty, forgiveness, loyalty, communication, buttressed by love and an abiding faith in the Almighty are the attributes necessary for each partner to enjoy life and to ride through life's difficulties.

Helping others gives the spouse a further sense of purpose. The non-physician spouse cannot cure diseases, but she can direct meaningful projects, such as encouraging medical students and helping them along the way. When George was discouraged to see bright, aspiring students who did not work up to their full potential, I suggested that we give an Award of Excellence each year to the student who had the highest GPA. We sacrificed a vacation trip to begin this project, but it has been very gratifying to see the improvement in the students' desire to excel.

The spouse should consider becoming involved in the medical auxiliary, an organization of physician's spouses. Medical auxiliary groups exchange ideas, do community work, and give scholarships to medical and nursing students, as well as to other health care students. They also lobby and influence legislators seriously to consider legislation that promotes better health care for citizens.

A wife may also promote the well-being of her mate by researching ways to help him. For example, when I read that golf is a good sport for taking the physician's mind off his often taxing work, I bought a golf set and asked a friend who was a semi-pro to take George out to the driving range and give him some pointers. George liked it and continues to play regularly.

Occasionally, one or more of a physician's children may decide to study medicine. If this happens, my advice is, "Do not push, but encourage." They should make their own decision. It is gratifying to see a child follow in the footsteps of her physician daddy. But it is tragic to see a child pushed into medicine and either fail or be unhappy because she was pushed into it.

Yes, the physician's spouse has an important role to play if the team is to be a winning one.

In a Nutshell

As a spouse to a medical student, resident or beginning practitioner, one should:

- Keep expenses down

- Encourage him or her

- Allow the quiet he or she needs for study.

As a spouse to a practicing physician, one should:

- Help at the office if needed

- Help him or her lead a balanced life and healthy lifestyle.

CHAPTER 20

Retirement

To the medical student or to the resident or physician beginning his practice, retirement seems light years away, but planning made in these early years may affect the timing of retirement. Too often, large debts incurred during medical education keeps doctors working longer than they had planned. Planning should begin while you are still in medical school. Sure, you like many, may have to borrow to pay for tuition, but don't compound the problem by buying before you can afford it, an expensive car or an elaborately furnished apartment, or St. John attire. In other words, don't spend income you haven't yet earned.

At the same time, within your limits live fully as you go along; don't wait till your later years to do all the things you want to do. Along the way, there is a home to buy, children to educate, places to travel to, and vacations to enjoy. I've known people who, sadly, put away most of their income for retirement and then developed a crippling disease six months after they retired. Obviously, it's all a question of balance and careful planning.

Basic planning is simple enough. Just set aside five, ten or fifteen percent of your net earnings in an IRA as you become financially able to do so. Engage a financial advisor or planner, since financial planning is often a job for experts. Have an emergency fund and appropriate insurance: disability, life, malpractice, auto, homeowners, a medical liability rider, and long-term healthcare.

Keep in mind that planning means not only preparing for what *you* want but also what your spouse wants. I learned that lesson the hard way I had a rude awakening when my wife, Lula, and I attended a seminar on retirement planning sponsored by the AMA. We had already done some planning by deciding to be ready for retirement at age sixty-five. I had seen too many friends approach retirement and become ill or die within a few months of retirement; so while I was still working we had traveled, educated our kids, worked in the community and in our church, and tried to live fully along the way. However, we had never discussed where we would live when I retired.

At the seminar on retirement, the director had couples express their hopes individually. As it happened, I went first, confident that Lula and I were on the same page. We both are from Florida, we both attended Florida A&M University, and we have many friends now living in Florida. I assumed that we would return to Florida, and in fact, I had bought property on two sites, in addition to owning property in Gainesville left to us by my parents. When I was asked about my retirement plans, I indicated that we were going to return to Florida and build a home there. I was surprised to see Lu, sitting across the room, waving her hand frantically until the seminar director asked what her problem was. "I'm his wife," she said, "and I plan to live in Indianapolis, where most of my friends live." That is when Lu and I began talking, and the upshot was that we remained in Indianapolis.

Where do *you* want to retire? Before you make a final answer, try it out for a few weeks in different seasons. While we were visiting in Orlando a few years ago, I was hailed in the street by a medical school classmate I had not seen since our twenty-fifth class reunion.

"What are you doing here?" I asked.

"Oh, we're here to buy a home, in fact two homes. One is for me and Hazel, my wife, and one for our daughter, Cheryl. We can sell our home in New York and buy two homes here and still have money left."

"Have you lived here before?" I asked. "Living in Florida is very different from living in New York. I'd rent a few months, especially in the summer, to see if you like it."

"Oh, we like it fine," he said confidently, looking around him. He had overlooked the fact that it was spring, when most places look good.

"How long have you been here in Florida?"

"We came in yesterday."

"I'd wait a while," I advised him.

They apparently took my advice. They did not buy a home in Florida and are now retired in New York.

Though finances and place of retirement are top priorities, there are other important things to think about when you are preparing for retirement. "Remember, when the phone rings, it's not for you," I was advised shortly before my retirement. It's true. Most of the calls are for Lula, and I've had to learn not let that deflate my ego. Such curtailments depress some retired physicians. "What I missed most," a retired surgeon told me, "was going out to see the family after surgery and explaining the surgery to them. It gave me a sense of authority, of power. Often there were five or more people who would be there attentively listening to me. Now no one does." When his practice stopped, he rapidly became an alcoholic.

Another retired doctor I know trudges each morning over to the doctor's lounge of the hospital where he had worked, pours himself one cup of coffee after another, and chats with practicing physicians or other retired ones. Then, reluctantly, after three or four hours, he goes home. Still another retired surgeon I know missed surgery so much that he asked other surgeons to let him assist at surgery. Other retired physicians help out colleagues by taking history and physicals for the group of which he'd been part.

These services are commendable, but they sometimes look a little desperate. Things change, and sometimes the best we can do is let them change. One way of doing this is taking up new interests, even before retirement. Hobbies can help. Depending on one's bent, that can mean woodwork or playing golf or bridge, or throwing or molding pottery or doing photography or bowling, or doing community work unrelated to medicine. Some people find satisfaction in writing their memoirs or developing a family history; others in volunteering at church or mentoring a student or serving on a nonprofit board.

Certainly, when we're retired, we need to keep busy—but don't overdo it. If you aren't careful, you will be in constant demand and become overworked because, as people will remind you, "you are retired and have plenty of time." Volunteer work return to you more than you give, but leave yourself time to relax, to think, yes, to reminisce, and to pursue interests you have not had time for but always wanted to do.

In a Nutshell

- Plan for retirement long before you actually retire.

- Be sure that your spouse and you are on the same page.

- Save money toward retirement.

- Work with an investor and/or a financial planner.

- Live in an area for at least a few weeks in different seasons before selling your home to move there.

- Once retired, develop interests to keep you busy.

Epilogue

To be a physician is godly, noble, and rewarding, but it takes discipline and hard work to get there. People want to become physicians for any number of reasons, but the most trustworthy reason is a burning desire to serve mankind by relieving pain and suffering.

If you are considering a career in medicine, the important question is how badly you want it. Once you've come up with a confident, positive answer, work toward it with an unwavering intensity of effort, in spite of the negative feedback you may sometimes get from counselors. In this book, we've tried to let you foresee what this commitment means. Are you willing to accept the challenge, and in the process help eliminate health disparities?

APPENDIX I

What's New in Medical Education?

Statement by the Association of American Medical Colleges

1. The Association of American Medical Colleges (AAMC) has recently written this revised definition of "underrepresented minorities" (URM): "Underrepresented in medicine [refers to] racial and ethnic populations...underrepresented...relative to their numbers in the general population." While the new definition, in the light of shifting demographics, no longer lists specific racial groups, "...the AAMC remains committed to ensuring access to medical education and medicine-related careers for individuals from these four historically underrepresented racial/ethnic groups": Blacks, Mexican-Americans, Native Americans (that is, American Indians, Alaska Natives, and Native Hawaiians), and mainland Puerto Ricans. (For more on URM see *www.aamc.org/meded/urm/start.htm*.)

2. The National Resident Matching Program has now issued a policy requiring that, prior to the ranking deadlines, residency programs disclose the program-specific contracts that residency applicants would be expected to sign after matching with those programs. This begins with the 2005 Match. (For more on Matching Program *see www.nrmp.org/*.)

3. According to the Associated Press' report in the *Indianapolis Star* (July, 2003) Medical students taking the National Board of Medical Examiners now have to pass a live-action test that evaluates their clinical skills and bedside manner. The test will cost $975 and be given in Chicago, Philadelphia, Atlanta, Los Angeles, and Houston.

4. Stanford University Medical School now requires their first year medical students to choose a "scholarly concentration." This is similar to a major. Other schools, like Harvard, are considering instituting the same policy. (For Stanford's policy, see *www.medstrategicplan.stanford.edu/scholarly_tracks/proposals.html*.)

5. The AAMC reports that applications to medical schools for 2004 increased by 3.4 percent. The majority were females— 17,672 in a pool of almost 35,000. Applications from Black women increased by ten percent to 1,904. All Black applications increased almost five percent to 2,736. However, the number of Blacks accepted to medical school declined by six percent to 1,956. Hispanic applications increased approximately two percent to 2, 483, but the number entering school decreased four percent to 1,089. (For more on these statistics, see *www.aamc.org/data/facts/start.htm*.)

APPENDIX 2

MCAT Update Announcement

The web site for current updates is *http://www.aamc.org/students/mcat/mcatessentials.pdf.*

About the Authors

George H. Rawls, a native of Gainesville, Florida, graduated co-valedictorian of Lincoln High School, summa Cum Laude at Florida A&M University and with honors from Howard University School of Medicine where he utilized a full Pepsi Cola Scholarship. After 2 years in the army, he completed a surgical residency under Ohio State University. He practiced surgery in Indianapolis for thirty-four years. He then became Assistant Dean and Clinical Professor of Surgery at Indiana University School of Medicine for five years before retiring and retaining these titles with emeritus status.

Dr. Rawls is active in his church and community. He is an elder at Witherspoon Presbyterian Church. He has served on the boards of the Children's Museum, Urban League, Goodwill, and Indianapolis Zoo. He was co-chairman of the life membership committee of the NAACP for thirty years.

Dr. Rawls has also served as president of the Indianapolis and Indiana State Medical Societies and delegate to the NMA and AMA. He has written three books and co-authored a fourth—*The History of the Black Physician in Indianapolis from 1870 to 2000; The Surgeon's Turn; Papa I want to be a Surgeon*; and *Managing Cancer: the African-American's Guide to Prevention, Diagnosis and Treatment*. He has authored many medical articles in several journals.

He has been awarded two Doctor of Science honorary degrees from Florida A&M University and Indiana University.

He and his wife, Lula, endowed a full scholarship at Florida A&M in 1989 and established an Award of Excellence at Indiana University School of Medicine in 1995. Health and Hospital Corporation of Indianapolis established a four year tuition free scholarship in 2000 in his honor (Rawls scholars) to be awarded annually.

Dr. Rawls and his wife Lula Pendleton Rawls have three daughters, and live in Indiana where he enjoys bridge, golf, reading, writing, and public speaking.

A native of Gary, Indiana, Robert Patterson is a graduate of DePauw University with a degree in Economics and Philosophy. Subsequently, he was awarded the Consortium Award for Graduate Study in Management and attended Indiana University in Bloomington, IN where he received an MBA with a concentration in Marketing. Upon graduation he accepted an opportunity to serve as a pharmaceutical sales representative with Eli Lilly and Company.

Dr. Patterson entered medical school as the inaugural winner of the George Rawls, MD Scholarship at Indiana University School of Medicine (IUSM). Dr. Patterson is an inaugural member of the IUSM's Diversity Council and served two terms as president of the IUSM Student National Medical Association.

In 2004 he utilized these dual positions to create a Diversity Week celebration on the school's campus which honors the memory of Dr. Martin Luther King, Jr. by focusing on minority heath care issues. Dr. Patterson's accomplishments have attracted national attention. He was awarded the American Medical Association's Student Leadership Award for 2003-2004 which acknowledges the twenty most gifted and energetic student leaders in the country. In addition, he was also awarded the Student National Medical Association's Member of the Year award for 2003-2004 and the Journal of the National Medical Association's Award of Journalistic Excellence in October of 2004, becoming the first student to be nationally recognized by all three major medical organizations in the same academic year.

Presently, he is a resident in psychiatry at University of Louisville Medical School.

REFERENCES

Cantor, J; Miles, E; Baker, L; Barker, D. "Physician Service to the Underserved: Implications for Affirmative Action in Medical Education," 1996, *Inquiry,* 33: 167-180.

Carlisle, D.M.; Gardner, J.E., Liu, H. "The entry of underrepresented minority students into U.S. medical schools: an evaluation of recent trends," *American Journal of Public Health.* 1998; 88:1314-8.

"Defending Diversity: Affirmative Action and Medical Education." *American Journal of Public Health*—Vol. 89 (8):1256-1261— August, 1999.

Hojat, M; Blackow, R.S., Robeson, M; Veloski, J.J., Bornstein, B.D. "Postgraduate preparation and performance in medical school," *Academic Medicine.* 1990; 65:388-91.

Koenig, J.A., Leger, K.F. "A comparison of re-test performances and test-preparation methods for MCAT examines groups by gender and race-ethnicity," *Academic Medicine,* 1997; 72(suppl): S100-S1002.

Komaromy, M; Grumbach, K; Drake, M; Vranizan, K; Lurie, N; Keane, D; Bindman, A; "The Role of Black and Hispanic Physicians in Providing Health Care for Underserved Populations," *New England Journal of Medicine*, 1996, 334: 1305-1310.

Lipscomb, W.D., Mullan, P.B., Zepeda, M., Price J. A Retrospective analysis of a program designed to facilitate the entry of under-represented minority students into medical school: program trends and outcomes. *Academic Medicine*. 1993; 68 (10 suppl):S10-S12.

McGlinn, S., Jackson, E.W., Bardo, H.R. "Postgraduate Medical/Dental Education Preparatory Program (MEDPREP) at Southern Illinois University School of Medicine," *Academic Medicine*, 1999, 74: 380-382.

Moy E., Bartman, B.A. "Physician race and care of minority and medically indigent patients," *JAMA*. 1995; 273:1515-20.

Nickens, H.W., Ready, T., and Petersdorf, R.G. Project 3000 by 2000: "Racial and Ethnic Diversity in U.S. Medical Schools." *New England Journal of Medicine*, August 18, 1994, 221:472-476.

"Racial and Ethnic Disparities in Health Care." *The Journal of the American Medical Association*. Vol. 285 (7):883—February 21, 2001.

Smith, S.R. "A two-year experience with premedical postgraduate students admitted to medical school," *Academic Med.* 1996: 6:52-3.

Whitten, C.F., Postgraduate Program at Wayne State University School of Medicine: "A 30-year Report," *Academic Medicine*, 1999, 74: 393-396.

SELECTED BIBLIOGRAPHY

The 106th Congress Act-Minority Health and Health Disparities Research and Education Act of 2000.

Byrd, M. et al. *An American Health Dilemma.* Volumes One and Two.

Cohen, Jordan J. "The Consequences of Premature Abandonment of Affirmative Action in Medical School Admissions," *JAMA,* March 5, 2003, Vol 289, p 1143-1149.

————. et al. "Definition of Underrepresented Minorities (URM)" *AAMCpercent20 STAT 11/3-11/7/03.*

Cohen, Jordan J. et al. *MCAT Update Announcement. AAMC,* 2003.

————. et. al. "New Match Policy." *AAMCpercent20 STAT 11/7/03.*

Congressionally Mandated National Health Care Disparities Report. 2001.

Health Link Medical College of Wisconsin 2002.

Indiana Minority Health Report 2001, Indiana State Department of Health.

"Like Doctor-Like Patient: More and More Patients Choose Physicians of Same Ethnic Group, Sexual Preference." *American Medical News*—September, 1992.

"Medical Students and National Board Examination." *Associated Press-Indianapolis Star, July, 2003.*

"Medical Students and Early Decision," *Associated Press-Indianapolis Star.* October 12, 2003.

National Medical Association 2002 Annual Convention and Scientific Assembly. Honolulu, Hawaii, August 3-8, 2002.

Patterson, Robert D. *Healthcare Disparities Among Minority Patients in Indiana.* August 6, 2002, pgs. 6 and 9 (Report to Indiana Primary Healthcare Association).

"Racial and Ethnic Disparities in Perceptions of Physician Styles and Trust," *Archives of Family Medicine*—Vol. 9(10):1156-1163—November/December 2000.

"Racism and Its Impact on Psychotherapy," *American Journal of Psychiatry,* Vol. 140:1605-1608—1983.

Rawls, George. et al. *Managing Cancer; The African American's Guide to Prevention, Diagnosis and Treatment,* Hilton Publishing, 2001, pgs. 4, 7.

———. *Institute of Medicine Report.* "Unequal Treatment." 2002.

———. *Indiana State Medical Association Report.* "Health Care Disparities." 2002.

———. *Papa, I Want too be a Surgeon,* Guild Press of Indiana, 1999.

———. *History of the Black Physician, Indianapolis,* 1870 to 2000, pp. 1.

"The Role of Black and Hispanic Physicians in Providing Health Care for Underserved Populations," *The New England Journal of Medicine*—Vol. 334(20): 1305-1310—May 16, 1996.

Smith, Eileen. Drkoop.com Health News. "Legislating Fairness in Healthcare." May 31, 2002.